Ticketless

How Sneaking Into The Super Bowl

And Everything Else

(Almost) Held My Life Together

By Trevor Kraus

PLATYPUS
PUBLISHING

www.plat.pub

Ticket required for entry.

Just kidding.

For my mom, who knew almost nothing of this story as I was living it. I didn't want her to worry about me.

And for all my English teachers. Their advice and encouragement — when writing school essays was the last thing I wanted to do — made this book possible.

Spin-move (v): to attempt to achieve a goal or complete a task without doing or possessing what's typically required to do so. E.g. entering a sporting event without a ticket. Ex: "The game was sold out, so he had no choice but to spin-move."

Spin-move (n): The act of spin-moving.

Origins: Explained in Chapter 16.

The stories that follow are true.
Some of the names are false.

CHAPTER 1

NLCS GAME 5: GIANTS AT CARDINALS

ST. LOUIS, MO

October 19, 2012

I had to sneak into the graveyard to see my dad.

He was there because his intensity became insanity. I was there, terrified of becoming him.

He had been dead for a year. The cemetery had been closed for fifteen minutes, but the St. Louis Cardinals were going to win the Pennant that night. The Cards had been the bedrock of our relationship. And I'll visit my father's tombstone whenever the fuck I want.

I was on my way to the ballpark when I passed the cemetery. Its fence was twice my height, with anti-climb spikes on top. But no fence is unclimbable if you're willing to bleed.

Under an overcast sky on a windy October afternoon,

I clutched one of the vertical bars and wiggled my left foot onto a horizontal one. I pulled myself up and stepped on the spikes with the rubber soles of my shoes. I jumped the fence, landed on my feet, and looked over my shoulder. I was alone and unseen.

I found his tombstone. Engraved were words that could have saved his life: Let It Be.

He should have been alive to see the ballgame. He would've left work early and called me four or five times while pacing his apartment: "I have a bad feeling about this one, Trev. I don't care for this lineup. Not one bit."

Then, suddenly, he would have become another person. "By the way, Albert's gonna hit three dingers tonight."

"You say that every night, Dad," I would sigh.

Those calls annoyed me. I never knew whether to expect Charming Dad, Crazy Dad, or some combination of the two.

But as I stood beside his grave and told myself I wasn't one of those people who talked to tombstones, as if the person beneath could hear me, I would have given anything for my phone to ring.

Before I left, I whispered, "Albert's gonna hit three tonight."

I climbed back over the fence as cars rolled by, and I smirked at the drivers who looked at me, wondering what the hell I was doing. I got in my car and picked up my friend, Patrick. We were both seniors in college. We drove to the ballpark.

I had previously snuck into Busch Stadium — and 10 other sports venues. I called the process a "spin-move."

I knew the glass, exit-only, double doors near the main gate would be lightly guarded; I had spin-moved those doors a year earlier.

Patrick and I strolled past them and watched the sole, patrolling usher. It was the same man from Game 7 of the previous year's World Series, and he was in the same wheelchair.

I should have chosen a different entrance. I know that now. It would have been more difficult, but I would have gotten in. As an immature 21-year-old, though — with my calves twitching and eyes narrowing on the target — I didn't want to take any chances.

I myself had been an usher at a sports arena. I knew he wouldn't get in trouble. I was sure he would have a good laugh while telling his co-workers about it in the break room. Besides, he was doing his job well. I was just gonna do mine better.

"How does this go?" Patrick asked. The doors only opened from the inside.

"We wait. Whenever those doors open, we sprint past the usher. By the time he realizes what's happening, we'll be on *that*." I pointed at the staircase immediately inside. "Then we haul ass to the upper deck." [1]

Before previous spin-moves, I told friends, "Size up the second line of defense, not just the first. Visualize how the concourse will look in five seconds, in seven, in 10. Know your escape routes and get to the top of the stadium as fast as possible." But Patrick's hands were

---

[1]   Security is, naturally, tighter at the entrances — especially before a game starts. It thins out the farther you move from the entrances. Therefore, the most important and consistent rule of my spin-move career has been: Get to the upper deck, fast.

shaking with nerves. He didn't need technical instruction; he needed moral support.

I put my hand on his shoulder. "Harness the adrenaline. Trust your instincts. Follow me. This game is ours." We stood next to the doors with our backs to the usher and phones in our hands, pretending to wait for a friend. Fifty feet to our left, fans lined up at the turnstiles to have their tickets scanned.

A minute later, a stadium custodian, carrying a broom and dustpan, approached from the sidewalk. He waved to the usher through the glass and pointed at the door handle. The usher nodded, wheeled forward, and pushed the door open. The custodian grabbed the handle and pulled it the rest of the way. He walked through as the usher rolled backward.

I moved in as the door swung closed, flung it open, and sprinted inside. The custodian was blocking the usher's view; I don't think either of them saw me until I was on the staircase.

I tore up the stairs two at a time, running close to the inside rail. I thought of nothing but the efficiency of my strides. I turned around on the fourth flight, when Patrick panted, "Trev, I gotta stop. Been smokin' too much weed for this." Our sprint slowed to a walk. I looked down over the banister. No one was chasing us.

"That guy with the broom moved out of the way after you went. And … " Patrick took a deep breath. "And the usher saw me coming. He stuck his leg out to trip me, so I jumped over him."

"He say anything?"

"I think he said, 'Hey!' when you went, but then he got distracted by me. Couldn't tell you for sure. I kinda blacked out."

We ducked into a bathroom. I took off my black

jacket; I was wearing a red Cardinals shirt underneath. I took the sweat-and-dirt-stained Cardinals hat I wore to every game from my back pocket, put it on, adjusted it in the mirror, and grinned at Patrick.

"Damn Trev, your eyes are blood-red. You been smoking too?"

"Not even a little bit."

Planning a spin-move, assessing security, and sneaking into a stadium — willpowering over the rules and getting away with it — was my drug. The adrenaline made me feel like the strongest and smartest person who ever lived. Like I could do anything. And a spin-move always made the game to follow more meaningful.

Patrick and I walked out to the concourse and looked over our shoulders. We were in, clean. I pumped my fists over my head and galloped aimlessly through the crowd. I patted other fans on the back and shouted, "Let's go Redbirds, baby! Wooo-hoo-hooo!" Patrick jogged behind, making eye contact with everyone, trying to convey, *I know he's nuts, I'm sorry.*

We found a standing-room-only area, and I paced while rubbing my hands together and looking at the scoreboard, waiting to see how the manager had screwed up the batting order. I said to Patrick in a jittery voice, "Doesn't it feel like something historic is gonna happen, just for us? We wanted to get in, we made it happen, and now, watch: We're gonna see something special."

"How about a perfect game?"

"I'd take that. But I think Albert's gonna hit three."

CHAPTER 2

The summer I was 14 and my brother, Connor, was 11, Dad planned a road trip to baseball's cathedral: Wrigley Field. Our Cardinals were playing the Cubs in a four-game series.

His second wife, Marie, let him buy tickets to only one game.

Connor and I each knew what the other was thinking: Dad was more fun without her. We hated when she told him to be careful with money and to eat healthy instead of taking us for pizza and ice cream. She had taken Dad out of his cozy apartment six minutes from our house and moved him an hour away, into a two-story home with a drafty basement that stayed cold, no matter how many space heaters we had running.

We tried to hide our bitterness because Dad told us she was good for him. We only spent weekends with Dad; he needed someone to keep him company the other five days.

Besides, we were going to Wrigley freaking Field. As Dad hung up the phone after buying tickets for the Sunday Night Baseball series finale, Connor and I shrieked and skipped around the kitchen. Dad said, "Fellas, this is a top-five moment for the Three Kraus Men."

We didn't have tickets for Saturday's game, but we still trekked through a drizzle to shag batting-practice home runs and listen on our handheld radio from Waveland Avenue, beyond the left-field wall. It was going to be the best sports day of all time for the Three Kraus Men — until the following evening.

We reveled in the music of the street: the rhythm of teenagers drumming on white, plastic buckets; the lyrics of vendors hawking shirts and peanuts; the bass of rumbling trains. I had only seen Wrigley from the outside, but it was already sacred to me.

After that season, the Cardinals would be demolishing their ballpark, my second home, to build a new stadium. I was planning to handcuff myself to a railing when the wrecking balls showed up. Sports were about history, tradition, and diehard fandom, and I thought anyone who needed an animation of clapping hands on the videoboard to know when to cheer didn't deserve a ticket. And yet, the front office couldn't stop touting the new stadium's massive, high-definition monstrosity.

I wanted to stand and stare at Wrigley Field and think about how I was seeing, hearing, and feeling the same things baseball fans had been experiencing for 90 years. But Dad was walking frantically.

"Hey, you got three extras?" he asked folks wearing Cardinal Red.

They shook their heads.

He asked scalpers: "Whaddya want for three?"

"$150 a pop."

"Too rich for my blood."

We lapped the stadium. His narrow eyes darted around, looking for ... something. After another lap, he announced, "Guys — come with me."

Dad loved reminding us, as the final notes of his favorite, obscure, classic rock songs faded, our eyes wide with astonishment, that he had never steered us wrong. We knew he never would.

He grabbed one of Connor's hands and one of mine and led us toward a fence that read, "Caution: Construction Zone." The sign blocked most — but not all — of a concrete path that led toward the stadium. Although it was next to Gate D (the main entry), the path was unguarded.[2]

I had no idea what was going through his mind, but now, as a spin-mover on the back-nine of my career, I can guess. He probably thought, *Worst case, what? Someone sees and stops us? We pretend to be confused. 'Aw jeez, sorry, we've never been here before.' No one doubts a guy with kids.*

---

2   I took pictures of some of the gates/entrances I spin-moved. You can find them, starting on page 338, in the "Extra Innings" section. The first one shows how Gate D and the concrete path looked in 2016.

Gripping our hands tighter, he lowered his head and marched toward the path. Out of the corner of my eye, I saw ushers taking tickets at the Gate D turnstiles. Then I, too, lowered my head.

Moments later, the sounds of trains and street drummers yielded to sweet, cheery organ music. I looked up; the gray sky had become a gray concrete roof. When I saw cardboard nacho trays and plastic cups of golden beer changing hands at a concession stand, I knew we were inside.

The construction zone had led us straight to a staircase. With each step, a few more sections of upper-deck seats became visible. From the second-to-last step, we saw the dark green ivy sprouting from the outfield wall. From the final step, we saw the bright green grass and wet, dark brown dirt of the infield.

For a while, we didn't bother to climb that last step. We watched the grounds crew drag their rakes through the dirt and listened to the PA announcer's smooth voice welcoming us to the "Friendly Confines" and reading the starting lineups.

Wrigley Field was perfect. It was everything baseball, and life, were supposed to be.

We found empty seats on the lower level behind home plate, and sat there before first pitch. During the seventh inning, Dad said to follow him. He took us from our good seats to great ones, five rows behind the dugout. An usher saw and asked for our tickets.

Dad stood up and fumbled through his pockets.

"Guess we lost 'em."

"Come with me," the usher said. He took us out of the stadium.

Once we were out of the usher's earshot, Connor and I glared at Dad. We had been happy in our original seats.

"Why'd you do that?!" my usually calm, quiet brother said, as he threw his hands in the air.

"I'm sorry, fellas," Dad said. "I'll fix this."

The scalpers were gone, and the ticket office was closed. Dad led us to the gate for the bleachers, which was flanked by three ushers wishing a pleasant evening to exiting fans.

"We were trying to catch the view from the bleachers … accidentally left the stadium," Dad blurted. Without waiting for a response, he grabbed our hands and speed-walked past the ushers. They stood still and said nothing.

"Well, boys, we'll be talking about this day for the rest of our lives," Dad said as we settled into our new seats.

We knew he was right. We knew he could do anything. And the Cardinals won.

CHAPTER 3

Before we were allowed to eat breakfast, we had to scrub the table clean, remove the newspaper from its dirty plastic sleeve, and wash our hands. Then we could make our cereal, always in the same way: Wheaties on the bottom; one-third of the bowl. Cheerios in the middle; one-half of the bowl. A sprinkling of Oatmeal Squares on top.

I would inch my arm toward the newspaper. Dad would pretend not to notice. I would grab the paper and he would lunge for it, and miss, a split-second later.

"Excuse me, sir, I believe I paid for that there newspaper."

"That's ok, I only want the sports section," I would say, knowing he wanted it too. He always let me go first.

My parents got divorced when I was nine. I didn't know why. All I remember is sitting at the kitchen table as Dad told us, with Mom by his side, in a clear, firm voice, "Daddy's moving out." My brother and I burst into tears.

Connor loved the Pokémon card game and TV show. Dad knew nothing about it, but said, "Fellas, it's alright, we'll still talk all the time. Con, you can call me up just to say 'Pokémon, Pokémon, Pokémon. Pokémon!'" We burst into laughter.

Years later, Mom described the moment the marriage broke. They were driving home from a St. Louis Rams playoff game — a 49-37 win over the Vikings, on January 16, 2000. Dad was black-out drunk in the passenger seat. He was upset for some reason Mom couldn't remember.

"He just started punching my arm," Mom told me. "I took pictures of the bruise the next day. It was really swollen."

I couldn't bring myself to ask if that was the only time he had been violent toward her. Deep down, I knew the answer. He had a bad temper, and anything could set it off.

After the divorce, my brother and I spent almost every weekend at Dad's "bachelor pad," which we called it because we stayed in our pajamas all day, ordered pizza, and, too lazy to take out the trash, stored the empty boxes in the oven. And we watched sports all day.

Weekend Cardinals games started at 1:15 p.m. By 12:30, we started "getting settled," as Dad said. He would fill his favorite glass with ice, water, and a straw. He bought packs of 200 bendy straws so he could drink without having to sit up in his recliner.

He moved the small table beside his recliner an inch to the left or an inch to the right. He placed the glass and the TV remote in the center of the table. He checked the thermostat, although it hadn't moved from where he set it the night before: 72 degrees.

This was his heaven: Everything in his world under control. It was our heaven, too.

We watched every minute of every game, because that's what real fans did. When the Cardinals weren't playing, we watched the St. Louis Blues, the Rams, the Missouri Tigers, or whatever big game, match, or round of golf the sports world brought to our living room.

If it was a slow weekend on the sports calendar, Dad would unleash one of his greatest talents: scouring the *TV Guide* for classics from his childhood — usually an episode of *The Brady Bunch* or a movie like *The Andromeda Strain*. Or we would have a "jam sesh" and he would introduce us to a band from the '70s we had never heard. If we wanted to play a video game or watch a show on Disney Channel instead, he would say, "Fellas: Have I ever steered you wrong?"

Sometimes, we would protest, but by the end of the movie or album, he would say, "Was I right or was I right?" We couldn't argue.

His greatest moment of "fathering," he was proud to say, came after the Rams lost Super Bowl XXXVI to the Patriots on Adam Vinatieri's last-second field goal. (Actually, it went through the uprights with two seconds on the clock, which, for some reason, kept ticking. To this day, the Rams are owed a kickoff and a chance at a Cal-Stanford miracle touchdown.) Dad, Connor, and I stared silently at the TV for a while, too stunned to move. The Rams had been two-touchdown favorites.

Dad eventually blinked, lifted his jaw, and said, "Boys, this is gonna make it even better when we win next year." He drove us to Mom's house where Connor and I tossed a football around the living room, almost-but-not-quite allowing ourselves to smile.

Mom was a serious sports fan, too. She played soccer and softball growing up, and her two brothers are football fanatics. Her parents had season tickets for the St. Louis Football Cardinals for 16 years, until the team moved to Phoenix.

Her father had a heart attack and died one November morning in 1993, at age 58.

When the Rams arrived in St. Louis a few years later, my mom, uncles, and grandma bought season tickets the minute they went on sale. Family tailgates were the highlights of autumn, and, I think, a subconscious way to keep him alive in their hearts.

But Mom's emotions, unlike Dad's, did not yo-yo according to the outcome of games. She knew she had to wake up the next day for her dull accounting job. Her two growing boys needed food, clothes, and a subscription to *Sports Illustrated*.

According to Dad, she told him after we went to sleep, "Bryan, whatever you said, I'm impressed. I thought they'd come home crying." .

I think he repeated that story so often to make up for his quirks. When he asked us to look into his nose to be sure he had plucked every hair; when he ordered "unsalted and undercooked" fries at McDonald's; and when he told us, "I'm going over there to toot," but didn't make it "over there" and clapped to mask the fart.

When I was months old, and he was rocking me to sleep with a Blues playoff game muted on the TV, Brett Hull swooped toward the net, slipped around a defender, and rifled a shot past the Red Wings' goalie. Dad instinctively threw his hands up to celebrate. I flew toward the ceiling of our basement, and, I'm guessing, was suddenly wide awake. My short life of pooping, sleeping, and vomiting probably flashed before my eyes. "I bent my knees, put my arms out, and looked you right into my hands," he said.

We liked saying he was "particular." His quirks were charming, in a way. They made him special.

But he didn't see us bury our heads in embarrassment when he would ask waitresses at restaurants, "Will you turn the thermostat down by half a degree?" He didn't see us scoff and sigh when we changed seats at movie theaters three times because the armrest on one wasn't comfortable, there was something sticky on the floor beneath the next, and we were too close to a speaker in the third.

He didn't realize how scary his temper could be, either. He would yell at us, with his face flushing red and his fists clenched, "WHO DRIPPED WATER ALL OVER THE FLOOR?!" as if we were out to get him. Someone was always out to get him.

He did realize I was becoming a miniature version of him: quirks, temper, and all. I would catch him chuckling with pride when I used a paper towel to open a bathroom door. With a soft smile and wide, adoring eyes, he would say, "We're the exact same person, Trev."

And that's the way I liked it.

CHAPTER 4

I learned almost everything I needed to know about sneaking into sports arenas by working at one — and by getting arrested at one.

I was a high school junior. I had never been to a sporting event alone, so I lied to my mom to get permission to use her car. I said I was going with a friend.

At the stadium, I plunked down $17 for a hot dog, peanuts, and soda, and wandered into a lower-level section to hear the tune about the flag they sing before games. I was supposed to be in the upper deck.

With everyone's attention on the singer, I spotted an unhinged, black gate that led to the all-inclusive, high-priced seating area behind home plate. I drifted over and nudged it open with my hip. As the song ended, I plopped into a fourth-row seat.

After three innings, I moved into an empty seat in the first row, beside the dugout. It wasn't long before an usher approached me. "Excuse me — can I see your ticket?"

I pretended to search through my pockets, then decided not to insult his intelligence. "Well, my ticket is for Section 441. But these seats have been empty the whole game. If you have seats this good and you're not here at first pitch, you forfeit them, right?"

"No, sir. Come with me." He escorted me down a tunnel.

I didn't know where it led, and I didn't care to find out. When I saw a door leading to the main concourse, I shook out of his grasp and ran. He yelled to a concierge, "This kid was in the owner's seats!" I opened the door. I saw dozens of fans — a sea of red I could blend into. But I didn't see the policeman, who grabbed my arms and handcuffed me.

As he pushed me toward the police room, I asked, "Is this an arrest?"

"Not exactly."

"I sneak up to better seats all the time ... don't you guys usually just tell people to go back to their seats?"

"At the Old Ballpark, yeah."

He took me to a holding cell, where I sat for the rest of the game. Because I was a minor, an adult had to pick me up.

Mom would have been forgiving. She knew that teenagers find trouble; she and her brothers liked to brag about how they drank their dad's whiskey and refilled the bottle with water up to the line he had drawn. But she was out of town.

Dad made sneaking into better seats at baseball games an art form. He taught me to scan for rows of empty seats from above, in the early innings, and to make the move in the middle innings. He taught me to look at cup holders before sitting down because, "Empty cup holders equal empty seats." He taught me to make conversation with the people around our new seats, to look like we belonged.

When he was young, he knew a ticket taker at the Old Ballpark who would pretend to rip a ticket while letting Dad walk through the turnstile.

Dad would have laughed at my "arrest," but he lived an hour away.

So I called *his* dad, whom we called "Pop." His unwavering sense of right and wrong had not been passed down to me or my dad. He came to the ballpark, found my holding cell, and signed for my release. On our way to the car, he said he had spoken to my mom earlier that day. "I thought you were coming with a friend … where is he?"

"Yeah, I made that up."

He stopped walking. "You lied?"

"More like a fib, right?"

Mom wouldn't have let me take the car otherwise. Gotta do what you gotta do. So what?

He was something worse than angry. He was disappointed. He took a deep breath, shook his head, and we walked to the car in silence.

When Mom returned, he came over to the house. From the basement staircase, I eavesdropped on their kitchen-table conversation.

I remember Pop saying, "If we need to use his college money for boarding school, so be it."

He saw a lot of Dad in me — in the way I would

fudge the truth and do things like slam hockey sticks on the driveway when playing against Connor. Pop felt my dad wasn't living up to his potential, and blamed (among other things) Dad's dishonesty and inability to control his emotions.

But Pop didn't get it — Dad and I were *sports fans*. We had seen college basketball players commit blatant fouls and throw their hands up like they were innocent; we had seen Bobby Knight fling that chair across the court; and we had heard Jim Rome on ESPN say, "If you're not cheating, you're not trying" too many damn times. We did whatever it took to get our way.

Mom said she agreed with Pop; my lie was a grave offense. If she had really believed it, though, she wouldn't have encouraged me the following week to apply for a student usher position at the Blues' arena.[3] I would have to travel downtown, alone, three nights a week.

It was called Scottrade Center back then, the third of its four (and counting) names since opening in 1995. Connor and I have made cherished memories there: pulling into our secret, free, hotel-employee parking lot where nobody checks for permits and sitting side by side in the second-to-last row, celebrating the absurdity of going to midweek games in January against Calgary, with both teams 20 points out of the playoffs. But it has always paled in comparison to the St. Louis Arena, the "Old Barn," which Dad called his second home.

---

3   I don't like using corporate arena names. They take away from the warm, homey feeling a stadium should engender, and they change so damn often that they would be obsolete within a decade. However, the names of the venues in St. Louis appear so often in this book that I found no good way around using their corporate names.

The smoke that clung to every ounce of air exacerbated his asthma. It took an entire intermission to get to the front of the bathroom lines. But it was hockey like it was supposed to be: dirty, gritty, smelly. The building rocked in the playoffs — literally swayed as if an earthquake were shaking its foundation. Dad and Pop had season tickets in the upper bowl in the corner. They had shared an interest in chess and piano when Dad was young, but the Blues were one of the few things they shared as adults, until Pop's interest in sports began to fade as he hit middle age.

Compared to the Old Barn, Scottrade Center (like most modern entertainment venues) is sterile and stereotypical. So when I learned the ins and outs of Scottrade during usher training, I learned about almost every modern arena.

Most of my colleagues were part-time employees in their 40s and 50s. We made just slightly more than minimum wage, so most of them had day jobs. At our pregame briefings, I sat next to a friend who was a gardener during the day, and arrived with dirt under his fingernails.

When I complained once about an assignment, I was told by our full-time, college-educated, suit-and-tie boss, "I hate to say this, but the fact is, you're replaceable."

We followed the rules and did our jobs well enough to avoid getting fired, but there was no reward for going beyond the job description: Direct guests to their seats and respond to complaints while being friendly and helpful.

I'm confident my fellow ushers wouldn't have minded the spin-move. Dozens of break-room stories — about fans throwing up drunk or running around, frantic, because they lost their phones — began with, "Hoo boy, y'all won't believe this shit," and ended in howling laughter.

The same went for security guards, our teammates in the guest services department. Also generally in their 40s and 50s, maybe half of them were big and imposing, but almost none were in athletic shape. They broke up the occasional fight, but they were meant to be a presence, not a force. Chasing infiltrators wasn't covered in training, nor was it in the job description. Even if it had been, failing to catch someone wouldn't have resulted in a write-up, "corrective action," or firing. The security guards, I am quite sure, would've said, "Shit — I don't get paid enough to chase punks around this place." And they would've been right.

Our supervisors supervised employees more than fans. They were part-timers, too, happy to collect employees' initials on sign-in sheets and to follow procedure for any problems that arose. They were neither paid nor inclined to do much more.

We ushers had to staff the turnstiles from an hour before gametime, when fans were allowed to enter, until the first period ended. Every six seconds, a new pack of fans flung open the doors, and freezing air streamed into the arena lobby. I wanted to yell, "Close the damn doors — I can't feel my fingertips!" Thanks to the marble floor, I couldn't feel my feet, either.

I tried to greet everyone with a smile and, "Welcome to St. Louis Blues hockey." The team was struggling financially (or so the owners implied), and even the smallest positive interaction might convince someone to come to another game. But no one is immune to repetition and misery, so most of us wound up mechanically reaching for fans' tickets, scanning them, and handing them back, barely making eye contact.

For important games, I would tell Dad and Connor which gate I was working. They would bring old tickets and wait in the lobby until my supervisor left. They would approach me and I would hold my scanner above their tickets but not actually press the button. They would walk in and find empty seats after the puck dropped.

Occasionally, strangers got past me before I scanned their tickets. The leader in a group of four buddies would say, "Freddie back there has our tickets." I would let the first three enter, then scan Freddie's four tickets.

Or, a mom would hand me a stack of eight tickets for her kids and their friends. I would try to count heads, but kids don't enter hockey games slowly and calmly. Besides, I trusted that no mother would be diabolical enough to sneak one past me.

Once, with a game about to start, a fan jogged up to me and panted that he had already been inside and left his ticket at his seat. I could have called for a supervisor, but the guy would have missed puck drop. No one would find out, and the supervisor would've waved him ahead anyway. I let him in. Following procedure wasn't worth the effort.

To be clear, guest service employees, most of whom were big Blues fans, were good, fun-loving people. They did their jobs well. But I don't think they fathomed that someone could love sports — and the atmosphere of a sold-out arena — so deeply that he would do *anything* to get in. I spent all day, every day, inside the mind of someone like that.

I didn't like taking tickets. I wanted to be released from my position at the turnstiles so I could see the game. But the best bank robbers are former tellers. The best hackers are former computer security technicians. They learn, by mechanical repetition, how the system works. Then, they exploit it.

My mind wandered on those cold nights, as I scanned ticket after ticket after ticket and saw fan after fan after fan enter the arena. I don't remember having an epiphany, but I'm sure I thought more than once: "There are some gaping holes in security. It would be pretty damn easy to sneak in here."

CHAPTER 5

On December 6, 2003 — I know because I looked up the details of that night's game — I was 12 years old and the only kid at my maternal uncle's dinner party. I went alone into the unfinished basement, and for almost four hours, watched Kansas St. blow out heavily favored Oklahoma in the Big 12 Championship football game on a tiny, black-and-white TV. As we were leaving, my uncle told my mom, "Trevor's so well behaved. Just put on a good game and leave him be."

Mom probably disagreed with the "well behaved" part, but I was proud of myself. I was independent.

In middle and high school, I would come home in the afternoon, retreat into my cool, dark basement, and sleep until Cardinals games started at 7:15 p.m. Afterward, I would play NCAA basketball and football video games while sinking into my couch, practically comatose. They featured crowd noise meters. When you mashed controller buttons on defense to pump up the crowd, the noise could force opponents into committing turnovers.

If fans could actually affect games with their passion, I wasn't crazy for being a diehard. There were other people on my level — thousands of them, in fact, who were willing to clap until their fingers hurt and scream their throats raw. I wanted to experience that kind of environment for real: 70,000 Trevors, working together, willing their team to a win.

Psychoanalysts would probably say my spin-move career has been an attempt to live out the fantasies spawned in those virtual college stadiums — Death Valley, Camp Randall, The Swamp — with crowds loud enough to shake the TV cameras. They would probably also point to the time Dad picked me and Connor up and, without having time to get to his place, talked his way into a vacant hotel room for two hours so we could watch the Minnesota Wild's first ever home playoff game.

"You guys, that crowd is gonna be unlike anything you've ever heard," he said.

Around 2:00 a.m., after video games, I would watch the previous day's sports debate TV shows: *Rome is Burning, Around the Horn,* and *Pardon the Interruption.* By the time I'd finished those recordings, around 3:30 a.m., the new day's newspaper had arrived, and I would comb through the sports section.

I then crammed in half an hour of homework. No one could see me do it. I had to be the guy who put no effort into school and had everything work out anyway. After all, I was *independent.*

Eventually, I would pass out and sleep for an hour or two before waking up for school.

Mom would often say, "You know, when I was growing up, I had a bedtime." When I got in trouble at school, she would say, "Maybe I shouldn't let you do whatever you want at home." But she never followed through. Once, thinking a man-to-man talk might help, but knowing Dad was more of a buddy than a disciplinarian, she asked her brother to sit me down. He came over on a summer afternoon around 4:00 p.m., as I was waking up. He sat beside my bed and said my mom worked too damn hard, and that I was making her worry.

I told him what Mom herself had admitted: That I got good grades and didn't drink or do drugs, and the rest usually sorts itself out.

I think her underlying concern was that I didn't have a social life.

I once ran into a girl I had liked in high school. "Do you remember our freshman year, I asked you to one of those girls-ask-guys dances, and you said no, you wanted to watch the Cardinals game that night?" (I didn't, but I would give my Ken Griffey Jr. rookie card to see how life would've played out had I gone to that dance.)

I wouldn't say I was "happy," alone, in a cold, musty basement at 2:00 a.m., as I punctuated my 20th consecutive video game championship by jerking off — either to *Girls Gone Wild* commercials or the porno I recorded onto the end of my VHS copy of *The Natural*. But I was comfortable.

After I got accepted to college, I started drinking, smoking, and going to parties. I couldn't avoid girls anymore, and prom was the perfect excuse to ask a girl out. I could play it off like I was reluctantly following tradition. I wouldn't have to admit that I had just recently started to feel cool enough to join the game.

Most of the hot girls weren't smart, and most of the smart girls weren't hot. Monica was both. She had long, golden hair, long, thin legs, and scoffed once in history class when someone argued that Truman was right to drop the atomic bomb. She wore a sweater showing a band called Streetlight Manifesto, which played a type of music called ska. I had never heard of either, but if she liked them, they must've been edgy and cool.

I liked her even more because she wasn't so far above me on the popularity ladder that she was out of my league.

"Well said, Monica," I would comment in our Socratic Seminars. I timed my classroom exits with hers so I could sneak in another question like, "Whaddya think about how Malcolm X has been portrayed throughout history?" I looked up Streetlight Manifesto. But all I knew about romance and prom came from movies and Disney Channel TV shows.

I asked our history teacher one day after school, "On Friday, can I come in early and write a note on the last page of a test, asking Monica to prom?"

The teacher handed our designated copy to Monica and she got to work without seeing my note. I tried to focus on my test, but I was more focused on the angle of my head. I had to be able to see how far along she was without looking like I was cheating.

When she finally turned in her test, she started writing on a scrap of paper, then passed it to me. I still have it.

"I appreciate the valiant/gimmicky effort (really, it was pretty surprising) but I'm already planning on going to prom with Zach, as friends."

I didn't know how to react. I hoped she wouldn't tell anyone about my note, and I wanted to get the hell out of there. I looked at her, nodded, shrugged, then packed my things so I could vanish when the bell rang.

"Dude," I told my friend Dean, "I thought the clever ask-out works every time."

"Eh, you win some, you lose some."

"Prom's stupid, anyway. The Cardinals have a game that night."

Prom came and went, but those last two words, "as friends," gave me hope. When the school year ended, I asked her to lunch, and she agreed. With time running out, as we were about to say goodbye forever, I heaved one from half court.

"You know, we've read all those stories in English class about crusty, cynical old men, beaten down by life and all ... and I don't know, the one thing that should be able to lift anyone's heart is the smile of a pretty girl. And, well, I might not be old but I'm definitely cynical sometimes, and I just wanted to say that you've had that effect on me."

She didn't know what to say at first. "Wow. Thank you, Trevor. I appreciate that. I ... just hope you don't mind if we stay friends, since we're going to different schools next year. If we had more than a few months ... "

"Yeah, I know."

I remember blasting AC/DC's "Moneytalks" in my car, with the windows down, as I left that burrito joint. If we happened to stop beside each other at a red light, at least she would see me rocking out, as if her rejection didn't bother me.

A few nights later, I told my friends the story while drinking and smoking in a dank basement.

"You should text her," somebody suggested. "See if she would want to casually hook up over the summer."

"I'm trying to be a gentleman here. You just don't say something like that." That wasn't how it worked on the Disney Channel. Not even close.

"Just do it, Trev. You've got nothing to lose," someone else said.

After five minutes of pleading, they convinced me. After another five minutes deliberating over language and punctuation, I typed out a message. "Hey, you're right, there's no way any type of long-term relationship would work. But if you ever want to fool around, the offer's on the table."

It was two in the morning. I didn't expect a response. One came almost immediately. "You're kidding, right? You realize you just undid the last two months of being so nice?"

Sometimes, for no reason at all, a replay of the Cardinals' Jeff Suppan hesitating at third base and getting thrown out instead of running home to score a run during the '04 World Series will pop into my head. My reflex is to punch my left palm with my right fist and mutter, "What the fuck was he thinking?"

I don't remember what I said after her reply. But even

now, in random, solitary moments, I wonder what might have happened if I had walked up to her and asked her to prom, instead of waiting for test day and trying to execute a clever plan. I remember how ashamed and embarrassed I was in that basement — and still am now.

I try to cheer myself up: *It's just one of many losses that will make it better when I finally win.* But I still punch my left palm with my right fist, wishing I could do it all over again.

What the fuck was I thinking?

CHAPTER 6

"We're gonna see him on TV at the football games with his whole body painted, yelling his head off," Mom told our relatives when she mentioned I was going to Mizzou.

But my first memory of Missouri Tigers football as a student is sitting on a leather couch, drenched in rainwater, staring at the party around me as music bumped from my fraternity house speakers. It was about a month into my freshman year, and to find the exact date, all I have to do is look up the night the Tigers blew a lead in the rain, the Blues lost their home opener, and Matt Holiday dropped a fly ball to lose a playoff game for the Cardinals. October 8, 2009.

I'd heard that if you weren't in a fraternity, you wouldn't have much of a social life at Mizzou, so I joined one. I became a pledge along with 28 other freshmen. We had to work for the house — clean, give sober rides,

serve meals — and coalesce into a unit to earn admission as "brothers."

One of the brothers saw me sitting and staring. He sat
next to me and said, "Hey man, what's wrong? I know
being a freshman and a pledge and all this stuff going
on — it's rough."

"They lost. All three of them."

"Wait. Do you mean to tell me … " he shook his head,
"you're this upset about … sports?!"

I looked at him and sighed. He stood up, scoffed, and
walked away. He wasn't a sports fan.

Part of me really was that upset, but the vain, inse-
cure majority of me was trying to establish a reputation
as the diehardest fan in a house with a lot of diehards.

A big part of the reason I chose AEPi was because our
president *got it*. He remembered exactly where he was for
Suppan's baserunning blunder. When he asked for my
biggest concern about joining, I said, "Being forced to
clean and do fraternity stuff during a Cardinals playoff
game." He answered, "Don't worry; I'll take care of you."

Still, I learned quickly that sports were a distant
second in the fraternity's power rankings. Even things
like grades, campus involvement, and philanthropy were
means to an almighty, glorious end: pussy.

Girls were often at the house to party and help with
homecoming decorations, so meeting them was easy. But
while the other pledges seemed like naturals at chit-chat-
ting that turned into flirting that turned into drinking
that turned into sex, it felt like a charade to me — one I
should've been good at, but wasn't. I wanted to wrangle
High School Freshman Trevor into a headlock, force

him to turn off ESPN, and go to that dance.

One night, I sat down next to a cute girl to help with decorations.

"Hi, I'm Trevor."

"Nice to meet you. I'm Cecilia."

"What's your major?"

"Education. How about yours?"

"Journalism. Trying to become a sports broadcaster. Speaking of education, I just read this piece in *Time* magazine about the new secretary of education. Apparently, he wants to institute a policy where states will have to compete for education funding. He seems to think it'll increase test scores by big margins." I probably cited some statistics. "You read that one?"

"Um," she said, scrunching her face as if to pretend the question weren't ridiculous. "I don't think so." I thought I heard my pledge brothers snickering at me.

One of them stood up and said, "I gotta go take care of some school shit." Still trying to impress this poor education major, I responded, "Hey guys, maybe we should clean up the language around the ladies, eh?"

My buddies rolled their eyes and one shot back, "Fuck off, Trevor."

I wish I had listened. I wish I had internalized the casual, joking tone in his voice. Instead, I spent the next four years doubling down on my Disney Channel failures.

CHAPTER 7

"You know I wanna go. I just can't," Al said, as I badgered him for the third time that day.

"Why the hell not?"

"You know why not. I got a test on Monday."

"And you're gonna study for six straight days? How many times can you read the same notes?"

"It's gonna be a hard test!"

"Ok, here's what you do. Tell the teacher your grandma got sick and you had to go home and see her. They'll give you a makeup test, and since we're not in fuckin' high school anymore, they're not gonna ask for a doctor's note. There's no such thing as a bad excuse to get out of shit you don't wanna do."

"I can't do that."

"Hell, you can study in the car … unless, of course, we're having too much fun blasting Zeppelin."

"It'd be a really irresponsible decision right now. I've got responsibilities, man."

I could tell he liked that word, *responsibility*. It sounded heavy and important. I thought the goal was to avoid responsibility as long as possible.

Al was my closest friend. He loved the New York Islanders as much as I loved the Blues. Like me, he could recite *Seinfeld* quotes for any social situation. Like me, he had adopted the show's sense of self-loathing: "I'm disturbed, I'm depressed, I'm inadequate; I've got it all!" was one of our favorites.

I admired him for his willingness to do his own thing, even if it made him look silly. We bought roller skates and a hockey net, set it up in a parking lot in the middle of campus, and played one-on-one as passing students stared.

Toward the end of our freshman year, my car got dinged by an SUV. Insurance gave me a free rental a few days before my Blues were scheduled to play his Islanders on Long Island, at Nassau Veterans Memorial Coliseum.

Al and I visited the Island a few times throughout college. The Coliseum defines the area. From the outside, it looks like a bomb shelter. The dark green seat cushions were made even darker by 45 years of spilled beer and grime. The concourses are narrow. But the Long Islanders I met seemed to take pride in the things that kept the fair-weather fans away.

I only knew it was the kind of great old hockey barn I had never seen, and that it might not exist much longer. Old barns are more intimate but less profitable, so they're not good at staving off the wrecking balls.

I wasn't taking no for an answer. "Al, you're talking like you're 49 years old with two kids, a wife, and a mortgage. Some day, we won't have the ability to drop everything and just hit the road, you know?"

He asked how much money it would cost. I slapped together a PowerPoint presentation that broke it down. The last slide said, "Tests, homework, and meetings only have power over you if you give them that power. Keep them in their proper place: as dreary duties to be avoided."

I put my hand on his shoulder, looked him in the eye, and lowered my voice to sound serious.

"Your other option is to stay here and accomplish all your little tasks. Study, attend your classes. Great. You'll have forgotten what you did with your weekend by Monday. If we go on this trip … you think you'll ever forget where you were on March 11, 2010? You're at a crossroads in your life, right here, right now: Which decision will you remember in 50 years?"

I paused to let it sink in. I continued, "You'll tell your grandchildren about the time you drove 18 hours to see a regular season hockey game with Uncle Trevor, instead of the time you … sat around and did the same shit as every weekend before and every weekend after."

A twisted, goofy grin came over his face. His eyes opened wide. "I guess road trips are a big part of the whole 'college experience' thing we keep hearing about, eh?"

I could see him reaching into his stash of *Seinfeld* references. "Alright, damnit, I'm in."

We left on a Wednesday afternoon and watched the sunset in Indiana. Somewhere in Ohio, in pitch-black night, "American Pie" came on the radio. When Don McLean sang, "My hands were clenched in fists of rage," I held up a fist as I sang along. Al was doing the same thing.

"How's that saying go — the world is your oyster?" Al asked when we saw the sun rise over the New York skyline.

"Yeah. Shakespeare."

"Man, all you need is a car and a friend, and you can make anything happen."

We tailgated before the game in the Coliseum's parking lot.

I'll never forget that first sip of beer. The nerves of using a fake ID to get a 12-pack; the joy of skipping class; the 18 hours of dry mouths on the open road; and the absurdity of doing so much to follow our awful teams; it all combined to make me feel like everything was right and anything was possible. The cold liquid hit the back of my throat and sent a wave of comfort through my body like a good massage. The world was our oyster, and our pearl was Bud Light.

CHAPTER 8

To earn admission into the fraternity, we pledges had to crawl on a filthy tile floor, organizing 50,000 Skittles by color, using only matches for light. We had set up an assembly line and were making progress when a brother came downstairs and said, "Oh, we forgot." He dumped a bucket of M&M's on top of our neatly organized piles. The other guys hated it. I loved it.

"Fellas, look at it this way," I said. "We'll never be closer than we are right now. Eventually, we'll have our different things to do and girls and parties and classes, but it'll never be the same as when we were down here cracking silly jokes to pass the time while we sorted fuckin' candy."

"So Trevor wants to be a pledge forever," a buddy said.

"Oh, you like cleaning toilets, do ya?" said another.

"You like sleeping in bathrooms?" said a third.

I *had* enjoyed curling up in a moldy shower and laying a wooden plank across the top of the stalls to create an extra bed. Seeing two friends asleep, squatting on the toilet, was hilarious. When else in our lives would we make memories like that?

I started to respond that they were missing the point, that we would one day be nostalgic for this moment, that the harder we worked, the better it would feel when we got initiated. But a fraternity is no place for philosophy.

Sex was the only philosophy.

Sex was also currency. If you had it, you were cool. If you didn't, you were a loser. In high school, I had been blissfully ignorant of my loserdom. In college, it seemed like every night I had to sit through stories of blowjobs in the showers and threesomes in the laundry room.

The night before initiation, the brothers made us pledges sit by candlelight and share our deepest secrets. There were stories about mental breakdowns and dead parents; expectations, fears, and dreams. But the one I remembered was the humblebrag about the time Nathan's girlfriend's parents came home as he was eating her out on the kitchen table.

Against that backdrop, my secret might not have been the most personal or profound, but it was the most embarrassing: I was a virgin.

We had to carry around little notebooks and write the names of the fraternity's founding fathers and the words to our theme song. I still have mine. Before "Candle Night," I scribbled bullet points for my turn to speak. One of them said, "Pledgeship is too easy … tie into virginity."

I think I meant: The harder it was to get into the fraternity, the better it would feel when we did. We already had decided admittance was worth the struggle, so why not make the struggle harder?

I'd tell them I felt the same way about sex.

The word *brother* was sacred to me. Before I left for college, I told Connor, "Listen: If you need something … advice, help with your homework, whatever … call me up. I don't care if I'm in the middle of a test. I'm answering the phone." If these guys were going to be my brothers, it had to mean unconditional love and complete honesty — even if that also meant telling them the full, terrible truth.

I wasn't just a virgin. Only 48 hours earlier, I had my first kiss.

CHAPTER 9

NCAA TOURNAMENT — 1ST ROUND:

FLORIDA ST. VS. GONZAGA

BUFFALO, NY

March 19, 2010

Four days after returning from Long Island, Al and I were sitting cross-legged in an empty garbage bin in the upper deck of Buffalo's arena, breathing in old roast beef and stale soda, planning to jump out when we heard footsteps. Either they would belong to fellow basketball fans and we would blend into a sea of people, or they would be a security guard's, and we'd have to run.

We had just watched Mizzou win their first-round NCAA Tournament game — with tickets. Now, we were trying to watch Gonzaga — without tickets.

In 1999, after Mizzou's season ended, Dad said to me

and Connor, "Fellas, having a team to root for makes the Tournament way more fun. Let's find an underdog and love them with all our hearts for as long as they stay alive."

We chose a team with a cool name and royal-blue jerseys, figuring they would lose the next day and we would forget about them. Twelve years later, we were still diehard Gonzaga fans.

When I told the story of our hockey trip at the weekly fraternity meeting, one of the seniors had sneered, "You're insane."

I didn't care. Al had posted online, "Trevor is a genius for making me go on this trip ... possibly the best weekend of all time." Now that I had a believer, I wanted to prove I really could do anything — and that a weekend on the road was more fun than trying to get laid.

Al, Bruce, Steve, and I left for Buffalo on a sunny Thursday morning. We rolled the windows down and turned the music up.

"Hey, what do you think the other guys are doing right now?" one of us joked.

"Oh, probably learning some awesome economic formulas," someone else said, and we laughed as loud as we could, not because it was funny, but because the freedom of the road made everything seem funny. When that day's basketball games came on the radio, we gambled road trip expenses — fast food meals, tanks of gas, cases of beer — on the over/unders.

As Bruce explained on the drive, Buffalo is proud of its snow, chicken wings, beer consumption, and the Bills' four straight Super Bowl losses — which united the city in suffering. There was no silver lining, though, when Brett Hull scored on the Sabres' sprawling Dominik Hasek in triple overtime to win the 1999 Stanley Cup for the Dallas Stars. "We're still pissed about that one," Bruce told us. "Fucker's foot was in the crease."

We arrived, slept, and went to the arena in the morning. There were two sessions of games. Tickets for the afternoon session, which included Mizzou, were cheap. But Gonzaga was playing in the evening session, as was top-seeded Syracuse, whose record-setting crowds lived two and a half hours away.

We circled the arena and asked scalpers about evening tickets. "Just trying to get in, don't care where. How about $50 for two?" I offered.

"Get outta my face, man. It's at least $300 for a pair," they shot back.

Scalpers are impressive specimens. No matter how hot or cold the market, they act like they have the upper hand, and they're convincing. They prey on casual fans who don't realize that everything's negotiable. I try to throw their fuck-you attitude back at them.

Two straight road trips had left my bank account hurting, so buying tickets wasn't an attractive option. Neither was missing my first chance to see a Gonzaga Tournament game in person. I figured the market would soften, and we went inside to watch Mizzou.

When my ticket was scanned, I realized: We were in the arena. If only there were a way to *stay* in.

When we got to our seats to watch Mizzou warm up, I surveyed the building.

A year earlier, I had worked the Missouri Valley

Conference basketball tournament at Scottrade Center. Between the afternoon and evening sessions, we ushers went to the break room to sit down, rest our feet, and have a snack.

"There's no way they can cover all this ground in, what? An hour between sessions?"

"Do I even want to know what's going on in that mind of yours?" Al asked.

In a split second, a fleeting thought become a fully fleshed plan. "Hear me out. After Mizzou wins this game, say I find a hiding place and camp out for a while. Once they let in fans for the second session, I come out and get lost in the crowd. Show me the flaw there."

Bruce and Steve looked at me like I was nuts. They said they were only interested in the Mizzou game. Al sighed and said, "You're serious, aren't you?"

"Would I joke about something like this?"

"Goddamnit, you know I can't let you do this alone."

The Tigers beat Clemson and the public-address announcer gave his spiel: "Thank you for attending. We now ask that everyone clear the building so we can prepare for this evening's second session."

Al and I were already on the staircase toward the upper bowl, where there's less security.[4] We heard the ushers shouting, "Time to head to the exits. *Eeeeverybody* out," as they shooed the crowd down the escalators. We kept climbing.

---

4   Staircases are usually safer than escalators. (This was especially true in Buffalo, where the escalators are in the main lobby.) There are more people on escalators than on stairs, and escalators only go one direction, so it's easy to get trapped on them.

"How about a bathroom stall with our feet on the toilet seats?" Al muttered.

"I don't think they'll do much of a search, but if they do, that's the first place they'll look."

We checked the doors to concession-stand pantries and custodial closets. Locked.

"Point of no return," I told Al as I tapped the toe of my shoe on the floor and scratched my head. "We're about to be the only non-arena personnel in here. They catch us and they're either escorting us out or taking us to jail."

"Hopefully the former."

"No shit."

We had almost made a full lap around the concourse and were approaching the escalators, where the ushers and security guards probably congregated. I saw a black curtain beside a section entrance.

"This might have to do," I said as I pulled the curtain back, revealing a big, gray garbage container on wheels, with brown gunk plastered on the sides and crud-covered cardboard on the bottom. We looked at each other and shrugged.

We climbed in, closed the curtain behind us, held our noses, sat cross-legged, and covered ourselves with Al's black jacket.

"What's this smell like to you?" I asked after a minute.

I could feel him looking at me blankly. "Mold."

"I was gonna say roast beef. We'll get used to it. Anything for the Zags, eh?" (We liked pretending we were from Canada, where hockey is on every barroom TV.)

We had enough room, barely, to avoid back pain. If I

catcher-squatted and leaned forward, Al could inch his
legs out in front of him and lean back against the side. If
we switched places every few minutes, it was only *mildly*
uncomfortable, and if we didn't think about the smell
too much, it was only a *little* stinky.

But time crawled. We whispered the lyrics to a song
we were obsessed with, "One Bourbon, One Scotch,
One Beer." We planned our futures: We would buy
neighboring houses in Thunder Bay, Ontario, with frozen ponds in our backyard and raise a couple of NHL
Hall of Famers. We talked about how a billion moments
and split-second decisions had to take place in exactly
the right order, at exactly the right time, for the two of
us to end up in a garbage bin behind a curtain at an
arena in Buffalo.

Al laughed. "If only I had gone to UNC instead of
Mizzou, I never would've met the crazy motherfucker
who wanted to do this."

"It'll be a great story to tell in 50 years, though."

"Where have I heard that before?" I sensed
his sarcasm.

Every time we heard footsteps, we held our breath,
but we felt safe until about 45 minutes had passed and we
heard a voice ring out, "Grab that garbage bin for me."

We simultaneously sprang up, opened the curtain,
and scurried away from the voice. After turning the corner, we looked back. No one had followed us. We turned
another corner and saw an escalator full of Syracuse fans
streaming toward the upper level.

We were just two more basketball fans in the arena.

It was not exactly what I would come to call a

"spin-move," but it was the first time I attended a sporting event ticketless — without Dad holding my hand on the way in.

We sauntered around the concourse, cackling with our chests puffed out. We ordered the Buffalo staple, beef-on-weck sandwiches, and told the carver to pile ours high. We brought our much-deserved rewards to a standing table that overlooked the arena. It was filling with orange.

"I can't believe we pulled that off," Al said between bites.

"They make this shit so easy, it's like they're asking us to do it," I said with my mouth full.

I'm usually curled up in a ball, chewing on my shirt, during Gonzaga NCAA Tournament games. In baseball and hockey series, when your team reaches the brink of elimination, you can prepare yourself for the devastation of the end of the season. In the single-elimination Tournament, you go into every game thinking you can win, and then the game starts, and every shot, rebound, and foul call is a heart attack. When you lose, the season dies so suddenly that it's hard to recover.

That night, though, the basketball was gravy. The real game, me and Al versus arena security, had already been played — and we won. The Zags won, too.

I was a freshman with mediocre grades, mediocre looks, and mediocre athletic ability. I felt there was *something* unique about me. I knew I was more intense than most people — in the way I could be at an airport bar with a random tennis match on TV, see a ridiculous 40-shot rally, stand up in astonishment when it ended,

and ask strangers around me, "Holy shit, did you see
that point?!" as they returned to their newspapers.

But I'd never had evidence that my intensity was a
good thing. Now, I had back-to-back road trips to New
York, in which everything worked out perfectly, precisely because I was intense and went all-in for my teams.

I finally had something to show for it. I was earning
a reputation.

CHAPTER 10

WORLD JUNIORS — GOLD MEDAL GAME:

CANADA VS. RUSSIA

BUFFALO, NY

January 5, 2011

Nine months later, Al and I were in bathroom stalls, attempting the same maneuver at the same arena for hockey's World Junior Championships.

Al, Bruce, and I had tickets for both the bronze and gold medal games. Security would clear the arena during the 90 minutes between the end of the bronze game and the opening of the doors for the gold game. But as the bronze wore on, I kept checking the time on my phone.

"They have to open the doors for gold at 5:30. That's set in stone," I said at the end of the first period.

"There must've be 10 icings that period … they're gonna have an hour at most," I said after the second.

Halfway through the third: "Yo, their 90-minute window to turn this place over is gonna be more like 25. We just gotta hide out for half an hour."

"If you guys wanna do your thing, I can scalp your tickets outside," Bruce chimed in. We gave him our tickets and found neighboring stalls. We sat on the seats, bare-assed, like we were actually shitting.

If security were to search the bathrooms, they would see our pants around our ankles, but with so little time between sessions, I was almost positive they wouldn't even bother. They didn't. Bruce sold our tickets on the street, re-entered with his legal ticket, gave us the proceeds (a disappointing $50 each; we had been expecting at least twice that much), and Al and I sat next to him on a ledge in the last row of the upper deck.

On the drive back to school, Al brainstormed how we should explain our latest adventure to the fraternity.

"Let's practice how we're gonna tell 'em. We gotta say we made, like, $250 a ticket … and we can say we were squatting with our feet on the toilet seats."

"What, you think the truth would make us seem like cowards?"

"I dunno … it's just not as cool."

"Well, whatever, I'll let you tell this one."

Those 25 minutes hadn't felt like an eternity; they felt like 25 minutes. This one *was* less cool.

I also considered how the guys would react when they heard the story. They would, naturally, focus on our profits. That felt wrong. Sneaking into games should

CHAPTER 10   51

be about seeing events we otherwise couldn't have. It should be about making memories, not money. I wish we had left and come back in with our tickets. Spin-moves should be driven by fandom, not profit.

I decided that if I was going to keep sneaking into sporting events, I should lay out some ground rules.

First, if I already have a ticket to a game — no matter how much it could fetch from a scalper — I can't sell it and then spin-move. (I did once give Connor my ticket to a Mizzou-kansas basketball game, then snuck in, but it was a gift, not a sale.)

Second, I set a minimum ticket price of $50. If I can buy a ticket for that amount or less, the game isn't important enough to warrant a spin.

When the Rams were awful and the owner was plotting to move them from St. Louis, tickets were dirt-cheap. I still loved the team, though, and I added an exception to the Code: If I'm sneaking in as a political statement — a middle finger to a team owner — he's not getting a penny from me, even if that's how much a ticket costs.

On that ledge in the top row of the Buffalo arena, Al and I were paranoid. After almost every whistle, I looked away from the ice and stared at our section's entrance to make sure security wasn't coming. So, the third rule became that I wouldn't spin a once-in-a-lifetime game for one of my teams.

I was convinced the spin-move was nearly foolproof, and I was convinced I could do anything. Hell, I once asked a local about the logistics of sneaking through the Israeli border and onto the Gaza Strip. But, come on:

If the Blues were about to win it all for our first time, the .01% chance of getting caught and sitting in a jail cell while the Blues hoisted the Cup would be .01% too high. Even if I didn't get caught, my worrying about security would distract me from one of the best moments of my life.

CHAPTER 11

When I was a kid, my first taste of a Cardinals World Series title wasn't going to be *one of* the best moments of my life. It was going to be the pinnacle of my existence.

Sitting in middle and high school classes, in blue, plastic chairs, attached to wooden desks by thin, metal bars — antsy on a sugar high from my lunch of two slices of stale pizza, powdered donuts, and vending-machine soda — I scribbled pitching rotations and batting orders in spiral notebooks. As teachers' dry-erase markers clunked against whiteboards, one mental montage was more powerful and prevalent than any other: I would jump, I would scream, and I would hug Dad as tightly as I could when they won it all.

The movie *Invincible* (2006), about how high school teacher Vince Papale made the Eagles' NFL roster, takes place in a hardscrabble neighborhood of Philadelphia. Papale's father, a blue-collar factory worker and diehard Eagles fan, has a heart-to-heart with his son.

"You know how I used to tell you about Van Buren scoring that touchdown back in '48? That touchdown got me through 30 years at that factory," he says. It was the most romantic conception of sports this purist had ever heard.

To say my daydream "got me through" middle and high school would be a Hollywood oversimplification. But with each passing year — as the Mets beat the Cardinals in the 2000 NLCS; as the Diamondbacks' Tony Womack hit a walk-off single to beat them in the 2001 NLDS, and my brother flung his hat across the living room; as the Giants' Kenny Lofton knocked the Redbirds out in the 2002 NLCS, while I listened on the radio in my bedroom — my daydreams of winning the World Series became more vivid.

I would wear my ratty old Cardinals hat the next day, no matter how many teachers told me hats weren't allowed at school. I would kick my feet up on my desk, hands behind my head, and sip an ice-cold Coke. I would run through the halls between classes, high-fiving and hugging anyone wearing red.

Sure, I would get in trouble. So what? The Cardinals won the World Series. My life, as far as I could see it, would be complete.

CHAPTER 12

As a freshman in college, I thought if you didn't schedule your life around your teams — if you didn't run around shouting after big wins and sulk in a dark room after losses — you weren't a real fan. You were a bandwagoner, and if your team won, your joy would never be as profound as mine.

To feel like less of a loser around the house, I thought of drunken hookups with random girls as bandwagoning.

On weekend mornings, my fraternity brothers would leave their rooms, shirtless and muscular, with ruffled hair and glassy, hungover eyes, followed by girls in last night's dresses, carrying their high heels toward the front door.

Our house wasn't among the "top tier" of fraternities, so we only had a handful of Those Guys. Houses like Phi Kap and Beta were supposedly full of them. "Phi Kaps get laid just because they're in Phi Kap," our recruitment chair once said.

That's what our house aspired to, but I couldn't help thinking: How enjoyable could those hookups really be if they didn't require you to put your heart on the line by committing to a relationship?

"I know I could get an easy fuck, but when I write that down, it sounds so shallow," I wrote in my journal. It was a defense mechanism, but there was truth in it. I wanted a girlfriend. Someone I could devote myself to. I would send her flowers — "Just because it's Tuesday, and you're you," the card would read. I wanted to pour myself out to her in love letters. I wanted to make her feel special every damn day. I would put in more effort than anyone, which meant it would be better — more mean-ingful — than whatever the bandwagoners had going on.

I met Amy in a freshman philosophy class. She was blonde with streaks of black hair, a few inches shorter than me, and had a great body. She wasn't in a sorori-ty, which I construed to mean she was an "individual," or something like that. She was also a hockey fan — a Chicago fan, but passionate nonetheless.

After a party one night, Amy, her friends, and I were running drunkenly around the rec center's outdoor foot-ball field. She realized she forgot her jacket in her dorm room and asked me to help her look for it.

She swiped her card to unlock the door to the build-ing. We turned a corner down an empty hallway and suddenly, she pushed me against the wall, pressed her body against mine, put her hand on my shoulder and raised her calves to match my height.

Her lips touched mine and my brain went blank for a second, or maybe five, but eventually I realized what was happening. I pursed my lips together, opened them a bit, and closed them again, to imitate the motion her lips were making.

It was my first kiss.

On "secrets night" at the fraternity, 48 hours later, I started the story by saying, "Well, I kissed a girl for the first time, and I liked it."

"What, did you expect not to like it?" the always-drunk-or-high loudmouth barked.

"Shut up, Timmy," David said. "He's just quoting a song. Trev, you might not remember this, but you stopped by my room that night and told me about it. You had the biggest smile on your face. That's awesome, man. Congrats."

"Well, obviously, I'm a bit of a rookie with girls," I continued. And I feel like it's the only thing that's missing in my life, ya know? I've been so lucky. Good friends, decent grades, good health ... I feel like if I could find someone I really like, I'd have it all."

"You will, Trev," I heard in the dark.

"Yeah, you just gotta let it happen on its own time," another voice said.

My fraternity brothers would invite girls to parties or to "hang out," but a few times over the following month, I asked Amy on a traditional date: dinner and a movie. I was stuck in the 1950s, and I knew it. But on a college campus in 2009, I figured that made me unique.

She seemed to be the busiest college freshman of all time — an exam tomorrow, a project due next week, a weekend out of town.

After our final exam, a full five weeks after our kiss,

I walked her to her dorm. She was packing for winter break. Snow was falling. The temperature felt like single digits. On the way, as we chatted about hockey and tests and whether our first semester of college had lived up to expectations, I was thinking about what to say at her doorstep.

I had this much: "I don't know what's gonna happen when we come back to school. But I do know that right now, all I want is to feel the warmth of a pretty girl's lips on a cold winter day." Then I was going to kiss her, walk away, and hope like hell she would be my girlfriend when we got back to school.

We got to the doorstep and I could feel my heart pumping in my chest and my mind raced and the world around me faded and my eyes found hers.

"I … I don't know … "

"Whatever you have to say, think about it and text me," she said quickly.

I said ok and we half-hugged, my right arm wrapping around her shoulder, and I stumbled away in a daze, my hands clasped on top of my head, Bill Buckner walking off the field at Shea Stadium.

I was sure it would torment me forever.

The only thing we sports fans love talking about more than our fantasy teams are the heartbreaking defeats we've suffered with our real-life teams. My favorite parts of those ESPN *30 for 30* documentaries about the "Bartman Game," or "Red-Right 88" and "The Fumble" in Cleveland, are the Cubs and Browns fans describing their devastation. They turn it into a competition to see who has endured the most misery.

I remember reading about a man in Toronto whose final wish was for Maple Leafs players to be the pall-bearers of his casket so they could "let him down one last time." On the NFL Network's *Top 10 Snakebit Franchises*, New York fan and comedian Artie Lange said, "I got into the Jets when I was young. Then I got into girls for a while, but ultimately, I came back to the Jets. Because unlike girls, no matter what, the Jets will *always* fuck you." Other interviewees on the program, when told their team was number seven or whatever, insisted they should be higher.

Sports fans revel in heartbreak. We want to be the most dedicated, the most cursed, the most miserable. Of course, I take it to the extreme. Part of me — the part that liked breaking my ankle so I could shed the crutches too soon and play through the pain to show how tough I was — *wanted* my failure with Amy to torment me forever.

I ran the slow-motion replay in my mind, searching for some facial expression or inflection in her voice that might indicate how she really felt. I found nothing, so I did nothing, except occasionally, when I was alone, punch my left palm with my right fist. How could I, the aspiring broadcaster, fumble my words so badly?

I didn't text her. I was too disgusted with myself. Besides, there were 280 miles of Illinois farmland and a galaxy of awkwardness between us.

When we returned to campus, we had another class together, but our connection no longer felt like it was building toward something. One Friday morning, I showed up to class still tipsy from the previous night's whiskey. As we were leaving, I said, "Hey, listen. I think we could be more than friends, but I'm not sure where we stand." (If only I had thought of that the first time!)

"I appreciate that," she said as she veered ever so slightly away, toward the edge of the sidewalk. "But I've been talking to someone else."

The overtime goal that swept the Blues out of the 2009 playoffs had been sudden and final. The puck hit the back of the net and there was a pained groan from the crowd before the organ played the "St. Louis Blues" in minor key. After 10 seconds, the crowd began to cheer, to congratulate the Blues on a successful season.

I sat with my elbows on my knees and my head on my hands, staring at the Canucks as they celebrated. I couldn't possibly cheer, but I told myself that this experience was necessary. It was the first-round playoff loss every up-and-coming team endures that teaches them what it takes to win it all. Someday soon, we would be the ones celebrating.

I walked home after Amy shot me down and felt that same optimistic melancholy. I had entered college with no experience, but I had already come close. I had tasted what a relationship might be like.

Now that I had a clear picture in my mind of what I wanted, I wanted it even more. More than anyone else, certainly, because I was the most dedicated, the most miserable, and I took it the hardest. But the pain would pay off — in hockey and in romance. One day soon, I would win it all, and I would be happier and celebrate more profoundly than anyone else had a right to.

CHAPTER 13

A teaching assistant handed a stack of tests to my row — second from the back in the 500-seat auditorium. I took one and passed the rest to my left.

I wasn't enrolled in that class. Jim, sitting a row in front of me, was.

It was a mid-October Friday morning during our sophomore year, eight days before my first true spin-move.

Jim was proud not to give a shit about things you were supposed to give shits about, like school, money, and girls. The desktop background of his computer said, "It's not that I'm lazy — it's that I just don't care." I wished I could have borrowed some of his indifference. I loved him for his honesty, and for the way he could pretend to be happy while believing life is misery and then you die alone. I admired him for the way he didn't let little things bother him.

He also loved the feeling of doing less work than any-one else and getting away with it. The night before his political science test, he asked me for a favor.

"Trev, I'm fucked in PoliSci. I think I have an idea, but you're the only one who can help."

"Step into my office." I led him around a corner, out of anyone's earshot. "What can I do for you?"

"Well, we're talking about a huge class in a huge auditorium. They won't recognize who's actually in the class and who's not. You show up tomorrow, get the test — it's multiple choice — and run back here with it. We get a crew to look up the answers, you'll text them to me, and I'll have my phone under my desk."

We were convinced we already knew everything we needed to know, and we saw school as a game. Every hour we spent studying or working was a point for the teacher. Every assignment, every test that we rushed through or phoned in but passed anyway was a point for us. Effort saved in the classroom could be used outside of it, for what college was really about: having the best four years of our lives.

So when Jim presented a chance to help a friend and feel the rush of getting away with one hell of a con, while sticking it to bureaucratic, ivory-tower aca-demia, I was in.

"I've had classes in that auditorium. There's a pencil sharpener in the back. I'll get up and," I made air-quotes with my fingers, "*sharpen my pencil* until no one is looking, then slip out the door."

I barely slept as Thursday night turned into Friday morning. Jim didn't sleep at all; he had been

honest with each other?" But it's clear to me now that we loved the game. When we failed, it wasn't our problem; it was the *game's* fault.

In fact, we bonded over it; our failures with girls overtook hockey and *Seinfeld* as the backbone of our friendship.

My fraternity brothers never actually made fun of me for my virginity, but in my mind, they taunted me. My only comeback was sports. After the Cardinals won the World Series, my baseball fandom had dwindled, but my hockey fandom had swelled. That proved it was a good thing I still had my first girlfriend and sexual experience to look forward to.

I just needed one perfect relationship with the perfect girl — one Van Buren touchdown that could get me through forever. It could end after a year. Fine with me. I would be able to cross everything off my relationship to-do list. Lovey-dovey, two-straw milkshakes. Jewelry commercial moments with her head on my shoulder. Tender, hand-holding sex. I would have passed the test by which the heroism of every man — from Don Quixote to James Bond to Charlie Conway in *The Mighty Ducks: D3* — is measured: Can he get the girl?

But after dozens of rejections and engaging conversations where I didn't have the guts to ask for a phone number, I found myself doing things that I used to enjoy on my own — like getting high and watching basketball or listening to music in the dark — and wishing I had someone to do them with.

I've always squealed with excitement when thinking about my third-weekend-in-March tradition: skipping school or work, tuning out the world, and being alone for four straight days with nothing to do but watch the NCAA Tournament.

When I saw guys holding hands with their girlfriends and thought about the other things they did together, I imagined my future — a future in which it was the third weekend in March *every* weekend, minus the basketball. For the first time in my life, I was not independent; I was lonely.

I bought a two-pronged headphone jack that I kept at the back of a drawer. It had one purpose: so I could lie on my bed, with a beautiful girl under my arm, as my roommate slept, and listen to some obscure but awesome record. We wouldn't need to speak; we were in tune with each other.

I knew I could be the best boyfriend in the world for someone. Wasn't I just more interesting ... deeper ... than Those Guys with the nice shoes and shirts? When I loved something, I went all-in for it. That was a good thing, right?

"Maybe you're gripping the stick too tight," Al would say when I got turned down or blown off.

"Just gotta put pucks on net, eh?" I would sigh.

For a while, Mom found Dad endlessly interesting. She once said she discovered some new passion of his every day — and he devoted kilowatts of energy to his passions. But maybe girls could tell that gripping the stick too tight was the only setting I had. Maybe I was *too* intense. Maybe they knew what Mom found out: that "interesting" isn't far from "unstable," which isn't far from "insane."

on my tiptoes.] Barry Sanders. Madden ... ya know, the circle button on the controller."

"Wait. You're gonna get into the game by 'spin-moving?'" He nodded his head sarcastically. "I think we're done here, Trev. Good luck with that." He rolled his eyes and walked away.

"It's only crazy if it doesn't work!" I called after him.

The more I thought about it, the clearer it became. I would choose a time before kickoff when there were fans in the stadium, but before it got too crowded to reach a full sprint.[5] I would wear a red shirt, to blend in with 85,000 Nebraska fans. After I got away, I would take that shirt off. Underneath, I'd have on my *Real Fans Wear Gold* Mizzou shirt. No one would recognize me as the spin-mover.

With this half-baked plan, I set out for Lincoln with Bruce. He picked up his ticket and we parked near the stadium. I surveyed a familiar scene with fresh, devious eyes — those of a rookie bank robber casing the joint. While fans shuffled along, chatting and lining up behind ticket takers, I observed the patterns of their movements, which pockets they kept their tickets in, and how long it took them to hand over their tickets and pass through the turnstiles.

My stomach churned and my jaw clenched from the nerves, but I had the thought I would grow addicted to: I was playing chess, while stadium security was playing checkers.

---

5   It depends on the stadium and the event, but 30-40 minutes before kickoff/tip-off/puck drop/first pitch is a solid guideline.

As I took a lap around the outside, most of the turn-stiles looked the same. I chose one that had hundreds of fans and only one stadium employee behind the ticket takers. He was a program vendor, standing on a wooden platform. He was about 90 years old. He couldn't have been less of a problem if he tried.

I marked the ticket taker from a distance: A woman, maybe in her 50s. Taking tickets is robotic. She would reach out, grab the ticket, bring it closer to her body, flick her scanner, look up, hand it back, smile, then reach for the next ticket.

I thought through the procedure: Pretend to look for your ticket. Get through the turnstile. Run.

I told Bruce, "You go in before me, and she'll scan your ticket. I'll run past you and once I'm safe, I'll meet you at your seat."

He passed through the turnstile and turned left. I strode toward the ticket taker, made eye contact, smiled, and rifled through my jeans. I put my head down to look into my pockets as I shuffled through the turnstile.

Only when the last bar of the turnstile clicked did she pause, ever so briefly, stand up a little straighter, and blurt out, "Hey, wait!"

I took off. No literal spin was needed, but the name stuck.

A spin-move on a football field requires gracefulness, timing, and downfield vision. It's crafty, unexpected, and high-risk, high-reward. Ultimately, though, it's in-stinctive. The running back sees the opening and just fucking goes for it. He commits his body and his mind, expecting to emerge unscathed.

I galloped past Bruce, then weaved through packs of fans in line at concession stands.[6] I remember running past a man holding nachos in a brown cardboard box with no advertising on it. I remember thinking, "What a great sign that this will be a raucous, old-school football atmosphere." That's all I remember; I blacked out as I ran.

When I was on the other side of the stadium — out of breath, shaking, still regaining my senses — I turned around. I didn't think anyone had chased me. I was right.

I strolled into a nearby section, removed my red shirt, and sat to catch my breath under the autumn sun. I called Bruce and we squeezed into his one bleacher seat.

"When you ran past me, we were right by that guy selling programs. He saw the whole thing happen from his stand. When he saw you run ... " Bruce giggled, then composed himself, " ... when he saw you run, he yelled out, 'There he goes!' You made his damn day."

I laughed giddily.

"And then, after a few seconds, he shrugged and went, 'Whelp, he got away.'"

I had figured it would be easy. And it was. But my shoulders twitched and my legs bounced for an hour after I sat down. I felt like the smartest, coolest guy in the stadium. I hadn't expected that.

---

6   Don't worry about other fans trying to stop you. They won't know why you're running and will unwittingly act as your downfield blockers. Even if they do know, they'll probably be rooting for you.

CHAPTER 17

"You're goddamn insane," one friend told me. "You're trying to drive through the night, see a basketball game in Denver, and then drive through *tomorrow* night to get back here?"

I furrowed my eyebrow. "Um, what, exactly, would be a better use of my time?"

"You have fun with that," he said.

I was addicted to the road. On my 18-hour drive with Al from Columbia, MO to Long Island, it was like time had stopped and nothing outside of our car mattered. The entirety of recorded music was at our fingertips. There was no fixed, 10-minute walk to class into which we could only squeeze a song or two. The speed limit was a guideline, not a law. We could stop whenever we wanted, pee on the side of the road, and eat all the fast food and gas station candy we could stomach.

All I had to do was want a road trip badly enough to make it happen. I could always talk someone into it. Gas was cheap when split in half, and I could copy friends' notes from missed classes.

Drawing up trips was half art, half science. I believed it took a certain, cunning genius: skillful budgeting, precise time management, and delicate verbal gymnastics to persuade people.

Secretly, I hoped my road trip reputation would spread to the sororities. Maybe they would want to meet the guy who dashed off to Buffalo and Toronto and New York on a whim, like a CEO or international spy.

"Why are you going to Denver?" girls would fawn.

"Business. And pleasure."

My business in Denver was Gonzaga's second-round NCAA Tournament game the following day. I swaggered through my fraternity house, trying to convince someone — anyone — to join me. I thought I had hooked two of the biggest stoners in the house. They backed out after Jeremy called his dad, who "didn't think it was a good idea."

Why even ask? If you don't, there's nothing to disobey.

I bumped into Dan, the heaviest drinker in a house full of heavy drinkers. He was, predictably, drunk.

"Buddy." I put my arm around him. "Let's go see some Tournament basketball in Denver. BYU-Gonzaga."

"I got friends in town visiting me," he drawled. "But, goddamn, do I love watching Jimmer Fredette shoot the ball."

You have to jump on any opening your target gives you.

"You're probably never gonna see him play in person if you don't come."

"I have had 10 … or maybe 11 … beers and six shots

of tequila. I'm not going to Denver." His eyes were glassy, and he had to lean against a door to stay upright.

"All you gotta do is get in the car, then you can pass out. I'm good to drive until morning. You'll wake up and take over for me."

He stared at the wall behind me with his mouth half-open, his impaired brain trying to process what I was proposing.

"We'll grab some McDonald's on the way. On me."

He perked up. Tempting a drunken man with hot grease and salt was a dirty trick, but all's fair in love, war, and road trips.

"You're one persistent bastard, you know that? My friends are gonna be pissed," he chuckled, "but fuck 'em!"

Before he had a chance to rethink, I told him to pack a bag and meet me in the parking lot. We hopped in the car, filled the gas tank, grabbed some burgers and fries, and hit the highway. It was a 10-hour drive. He was comatose by minute three.

Al called as we were closing in on the Missouri border.

"Trev, turn around," he shouted.

"Why?"

"That girl I was waiting for at the bar never showed up. Got no prospects. No conceivable reason to wake up in the morning. Gill's drunk and depressed, too. So we called for a sober driver to take us home and joked about whether he wanted to take us to Denver. He said sure, and now we're on the highway!"

I pulled over, and they caught up. I left my car at an abandoned gas station in the middle of nowhere, and the sober driver took the wheel all night. We arrived in

Denver at noon the next day. We saw the Zags. Fredette went 7-for-12 from behind the arc for BYU. I kicked a folding chair. The Zags lost, but at least I had given everything a fan could give.

Not long thereafter, I was wandering from fraternity room to room at 2:30 a.m., trying to gather a crew to see the Blues play 17 hours later in Chicago, which was seven hours away. Kevin was a fellow night owl and from Chicago.

"I'm not a big enough hockey fan to justify it," he said. "It would be like if I asked you to take a trip to an NBA game." Fair enough. I would come back to him.

My friend Eric was a hockey fan, but an even bigger Cubs fan. When I mentioned the trip, he blurted, "What if we could catch the Cubs game in the afternoon?"

I smiled. "We can do whatever the fuck we want."

"Only thing is, I've got this meeting for a group project tomorrow. And I've already been a … less than ideal member of the group."

"That's easy," I said. "Just say you've got a very important family event you have to be in Chicago for. We're brothers, technically. Tell 'em confidently; they won't call your bluff. It's not a lie if you believe it."

He exhaled. "I can't pass this up." Then I burst into Kevin's room. Wrigley Field was his favorite place in the world.

"Updated, more epic plan. Drive through the night, we take turns sleeping, we get to Chicago in time to have pizza for lunch, Cubs game, dinner, hockey game, and we head home."

We pulled it off to perfection.

CHAPTER 18

I pretended to be clueless in my statistics class.

The year before, not long after attempting to flirt by citing *Time* magazine, I got surprising news: Cecilia, the education major, had been about to invite me to a sorority date party before she learned I would be at the lake with my fellow pledges for "walk-out" (i.e. binge-drinking) that same weekend.

I didn't think much of it at the time. I'd just had my first kiss with Amy and was all-in for her. When I found myself sitting next to Cecilia in that sophomore stats class, though, I thought about it plenty. Maybe I hadn't made a fool of myself after all.

She called herself clumsy and forgetful, and I would have thought her a ditzy sorority stereotype if I didn't know she was a straight-A student. Luckily, she was willing to help me with statistics when I pretended not to understand a thing.

As I got to know her better, I learned how street-smart

she was, too. At a football game once, with the whole student section standing on cold, metal bleachers, she flattened an empty box of popcorn. That thin sliver of cardboard was a game-changer for our feet and knees.

We wrote on each other's notebooks while the teacher was talking. After class, she would sometimes walk me halfway to my next one or I'd go halfway to hers — even though they were on opposite sides of campus. She liked that I wore my Blues jersey on gamedays.

"It's never a bad thing to be passionate about something," she said. "What's the point if you don't care?"

That was the sign I was looking for: cheerful, casual optimism about something I took much too seriously. A sign that she found me *interesting*, not crazy.

One Saturday night, she asked to borrow a Blues jersey for a sports-themed fraternity party. It came down to her knees. She looked at me and scrunched her face and smiled and laughed. I had to take a sip of beer and remember that she had a boyfriend to stop myself from kissing her right then and there. There is nothing hotter than a pretty girl in your favorite team's jersey.

We spent the whole party talking. After she left, I drank myself into oblivion, because I didn't know what else to do. The next afternoon, Al woke me up.

"Trev, you gotta hear this. Cecilia came back to the party last night after you passed out and we had a little chat. I told her, 'You've got my buddy tied up in knots, ya know.'"

"That's good, that's brilliant! What did she say?"

"She really likes you too, and she's not exactly thrilled with her current relationship."

I blinked and took a deep breath. A pretty girl, who I liked, actually liked me — and I didn't have to guess. I had proof.

"What should I do?"

"You should write her a letter. You don't have to send it, but get your feelings down. I did something similar once. It'll help."

At 4:47 a.m. on a quiet, snowy morning, after everyone else had gone to bed, I flipped on my desk lamp and sat down. If ever there was a time to channel my loneliness, frustration, and confusion into the keyboard, this was it. I was ready to show her the only side of me I liked: the one my friends saw on road trips. The one who spin-moved. The one who poured his heart and soul into the things he loved. The one who knew what he wanted and went for it.

I took a deep breath, glared for a second at the blinking cursor, and typed, "Hi Cecilia."

I rambled for a bit — it wasn't a Shakespeare sonnet, but it was honest, and then I found the words I was looking for, the ones that said I'm all-in, I'm yours if you want me.

"It's hard for me to be reminded so frequently of your awesomeness and still be burdened with the knowledge that someone else gets to take you out, hold doors open for you, offer you his jacket when you're cold, and kiss you spontaneously, just because you unleashed one of your trademark, light-up-a-room smiles."

I quoted Wayne Gretzky about how you miss 100% of the shots you don't take.

scored again, and when you're a sports fan who's been disappointed by his team, year after year, you feel it's over long before the game ends. Even your all-in rooting — which you're convinced can affect games — is powerless.

Yadier Molina flied out to right. I held myself together for a second. I was in high school now, and there's no crying in baseball. But then I thought about leaving the ballpark earlier that postseason with Mom, after a win against the Padres, on a sunny fall afternoon. I had looked over my shoulder as I walked out of my section. One last glimpse of my second home.

It was still beautiful, and perfectly functional, but they would demolish it, brick by painful brick, and I would never celebrate the World Series there.

Dad called and heard me pick up, but neither of us spoke. The dam burst. I soaked the mic of our landline phone in tears, again, as I watched the Astros pour out of the dugout to celebrate.

Two silent minutes later, I said goodbye. He said to call him tomorrow, and we hung up.

When I got home from school the following afternoon, I called and we were silent again for a long time.

"Trev, I think this is rock-bottom," he finally said.

"It is."

"But maybe you have to hit rock-bottom before you can appreciate what the mountaintop feels like."

"Will they ever do it?"

"I don't know, son. But I know it only takes one championship and all this pain goes away."

You never get used to the ups and downs.

Three days earlier, the Cardinals had been down by

two and down to their last strike. The season — and the
Old Ballpark — would die in Houston. I was, as usual,
in my basement, commiserating with Dad on the phone.
David Eckstein singled. Edmonds walked. The season
was on Albert's shoulders. The Machine. El Hombre.
The best hitter on the planet.
He sent an 0-1 slider into orbit.
I jumped and threw my hands up and the phone flew
into the ceiling. After running around the basement
screaming for a few minutes, I called Dad back. He had
almost broken his phone, too. Like father, like son, he
probably said.

I had been screaming so loud — six, seven, maybe
twenty-five bellows that came from deep in my stomach
and each lasted as long as I could hold my breath — that
Mom, two floors above, stormed down the stairs.

"Trevor. You have to settle down."

"What?" I hyperventilated.

"You're gonna wake the neighbors."

"WOOOOOHOOOOO-HOOOOO!" My voice was
raspy, my face was bright red, and my eyes were bulging.

"Alright, that's enough."

"Mom, are you seriously trying to ruin this for me?"

"You're starting to remind me of someone," she said as
she climbed the stairs and slammed the basement door.

I still thought that was a good thing. I wanted to
be like him.

CHAPTER 20

THE BORDER WAR:

NO. 19 MISSOURI AT NO. 2 KANSAS

LAWRENCE, KS

February 7, 2011

Jim was covering the Mizzou-kU basketball game for the student newspaper in February of our sophomore year. He offered me a ride to Lawrence, ks. (We use the lowercase; fuck kansas, they don't deserve a capital letter.[8])

"You know about the old Mizzou coach, Norm Stewart?" I asked. "Supposedly, he didn't let the team bus driver make stops for food or gas in kansas. Had to take care of that in Missouri so they wouldn't contribute to the enemy's economy."

---

8   I don't *actually* think this, but rivalries are fun.

"You could pull a Norm if you pack a few PB&J's and do your spin ... thing." I had only spin-moved twice at that point, but I almost punched him for disrespecting my baby.

Phog Allen Fieldhouse was the scariest place in college basketball. Iconic. Historic. Ear-splittingly loud. I was scared of it myself and almost turned down Jim's offer. It would be tougher to get lost in a crowd of 16,000 than it had been at 85,000-seat Memorial Stadium in Nebraska.

But I had to follow my own philosophy: Which decision would I remember in 50 years?

I wore a black button-down shirt over a blue long-sleeve shirt, over my Mizzou gold. At the media entrance, where Jim's credential was waiting, glass double doors opened into the arena. I went first. A step inside the doors, an usher asked to examine my briefcase, which I had stuffed with old notebooks and newspapers.[9] I kept thinking about a line from the movie *Catch Me If You Can*: "You know why the Yankees always win? The other teams can't take their eyes off the pinstripes." Just breathe, be calm, and look like you belong.

To the left, a few feet past the usher, two students in collared, blue, kansas shirts sat behind a white folding table, handing credentials to media personnel. They were probably part-time interns with the same level of "dedication" to their jobs I had to mine at Scottrade

---

9   Many sports gatecrashers dress up in costumes to get into games. I prefer to keep things simpler, but if you're planning a spin, might as well bring a suit and tie or a disguise of some kind in the car. Can't hurt to have an extra club in the bag.

Center: They were there to watch basketball games for free and put "kansas University Athletic Department" on their résumés.

The usher returned my briefcase. I smiled and thanked him. I took a long stride toward the concourse and away from the interns. Then another. Then another.

I turned a corner, stepped into a bathroom, and shed my button-down shirt. I dropped the briefcase into a trashcan. I left the bathroom and looked left, then right, then left again. I almost hoped some security guard would be running at me, just for the challenge. It had been too easy.

When I met up with Jim later, he told me, "One of those interns asked about you. I said, 'Ah, he's a photographer,' and that was it."

I found the Mizzou section and wanted to rip off my blue shirt like Andy Dufresne in *The Shawshank Redemption* rips off his prison uniform after crawling out of that sewer pipe. In reality, I wrestled it over my head, exposing my bare stomach and chest to the whole section. Out of 16,000 fans, I was one of about 19 wearing gold.

Moments before tip-off, the scoreboard decibel meter hit 117. Around 120, the sensation of hearing becomes pain for the average person. I sat in an upper corner of the arena as the videoboard played a clip from *The Outlaw Josey Wales* about how "nothing good comes from Missouri." It whipped the crowd into a frenzy, and "Thunderstruck" blared from the speakers. The students jumped and chanted in unison as the players assembled around midcourt. The other fans were standing, clapping, and yelling, like an army that had its enemy surrounded and was closing in for the kill.[10]

This is what I came for.

The Tigers were eaten alive, but the environment was the attraction. KU (just this once) fans went nuts from the opening tip until the final buzzer.

Before I left, I looked up at the rafters and read the famous banner, in medieval-torture font: "PAY HEED, ALL WHO ENTER."

I entered, alright. And heed was all I paid to fucking kansas.

---

10   In the ESPN 30-for-30 *Miller Time*, Ahmad Rashad remembered Game 6 of the 1994 Eastern Conference Finals between the Pacers — who had never reached the Finals — and Knicks, which took place at Market Square Arena in Indianapolis. "There was an edge to those fans like no other place in the country ... Looking up in the stands and looking at the faces of the people when they yelled and it was just ... " he scrunched his face, gritted his teeth, and narrowed his eyes ... "AGGGHHHH." Pacers announcer Mark Boyle said, "It was like a bunch of hungry people with raw meat at their fingertips."

There are three ingredients that can contribute to a next-level atmosphere like that. First, high stakes, of course; either a rivalry game or a crucial playoff game (ideally both). Second, a fanbase on the verge of a new frontier, like reaching the Finals or winning a title for the first time ... or the first time in decades. Third, a venue built before modern fire codes forced teams to build stadiums with seating arrangements stacked less upward and more outward.

CHAPTER 21

"I have a letter for you," Rachel, our go-between, texted me.

I was back from Buffalo. While inhaling chicken wings, watching hockey, and drinking beer on the trip, I hardly thought about Cecilia.

But she was *all* I thought about while brushing my teeth and tying my shoes.

If I had received a letter like she did, I'd have been thrilled. But maybe I had thrown a wrench into her life. Maybe she was scared by how strongly I felt about her. What if she didn't grow up in the 1950s? Maybe I would blink and 30 years would pass and I would still be waiting for a response, unable to forget or move on.

When I got that text, I allowed myself a fantasy. We were holding hands and walking through the park. I was leaning in, whispering something in her ear, and she was looking up at me as if she couldn't believe what I was saying. She wasn't sure she wanted to. She wasn't sure she wanted to be with a guy who had just driven through the night to see a ballgame, snuck into the stadium, then driven back in time to cheat on his test — and ace it. But there she was, holding *my* hand, because she knew she'd never meet anyone else with such good stories to tell.

I placed the bright pink envelope in the middle of my dark brown desk. I was afraid to open it. If I left it there, I wouldn't have to read the words that would kill my fantasy.

I showered and folded laundry as I waited for Al and Jim to come home. They had to read it first. If it didn't say what I wanted, they could rip it to shreds and tell me they loved me and always would. They read it, looked at each other, and handed it to me. I took a deep breath.

"I obviously have not done a very good job at hiding that yes, I am very attracted to you. When I break up with my boyfriend, you will definitely be the first guy I will want to go out with."

Al stopped me. "*When*, not *if* — that's huge."

I sat back in my chair. It was going to happen, eventually. I was almost happy she was loyal to her boyfriend. When I inevitably screwed up, maybe she would be that loyal to me.

"I am in no way implying that you will not have already found someone new. I mean with your good looks and charm, how could you not have? In which case I will be missing out on the opportunity to be with one of the most genuine guys here on Mizzou's campus."

After what seemed like months without a smile, I tried — and failed — to suppress one.

"You should see your face right now," Al said.

In one phrase, she had validated my entire personality. It wasn't impossible for someone to be attracted to my idiosyncrasies. I wasn't crazy, or too intense; I was *genuine*.

She said not to wait, but all the waiting — all the hours cursing myself for being superficial, neurotic, and picky, and for taking the game too seriously and being unable or unwilling to change — *the waiting* would make it satisfying.

Cecilia and I met the next day. I had jotted some bullet points on a notecard:

-Good to know we're on the same wavelength and not into silly little games

-Attraction is delicate, so let's stay friends for now but continue to be honest with each other

-End with a hug to avoid awkwardness

She giggled when she saw me take the notecard from my pocket to double-check that I had covered everything. Then she took a deep breath and said something like, "I'm relieved to hear all of that, and I think it's great that we can keep being friends, keep being attracted to each other, and keep being open." We hugged and smiled before I turned and walked away.

But I knew the next time we saw each other, we would find out if we really could stay friends for now. It was a week later, at a fraternity "beer-b-q." Al had volunteered to be my icebreaker. When he saw me say hi to Cecilia, he hustled over. He pretended to be drunker than he was and said, "Well if it isn't the penpals of Greektown. Ya know, there's a fax machine in the library if you wanna communicate a little faster."

In high school, I wrote an essay about Dad and his ... issues, knowing only my English teacher would see it. I didn't like talking about anything personal because talking about it was a sign of weakness. I could rub some dirt on it and get back out there. I especially didn't want to talk about him. We were so similar that it would have felt like talking about myself.

The only time I remember discussing his instability took place at a public library when I was five years old. It was just Pop and me. He drew a circle: my dad. Then he drew an arrow toward it from above. "This is me," he said. He drew another arrow from below. "This is you, Trev."

My father was a gravitational force — the Earth — capable of spiraling out of control at any time. We had to be the Sun and the Moon, making sure he kept his balance.

I don't remember how I reacted, or if I even knew what gravity was. I'm sure I was proud that Pop had spoken to me like an adult. I probably pretended to understand what he was saying, to appear mature.

Pop wound up supporting Dad financially. He spent hundreds of hours on the phone, counseling him through anxieties, encouraging him to take medicine, and suggesting that he be honest with his psychiatrists. Pop fulfilled his role. I fulfilled mine as long as I could. Eventually, though, I just wanted Dad to stop calling.

Yet, there I was, in the fraternity living room at something called a beer-b-q, not even drunk yet, talking about the specter of my father for the first time in 15 years. I told Cecilia my deepest, most personal fear: "He's just ... not well. He's done a lot of bad things. And I'm terrified I'll wind up just like him." I knew I could tell her anything, and I knew she would have the perfect response. She didn't let me down.

"The fact that you realize it means you won't, don't ya think?"

I wonder now if it wasn't Cecilia herself I was attracted to. Maybe it was the way she could ease my mind with one sentence, one smile, and one shrug.

We flirted over text message almost every day for the rest of the semester, usually with lots of smiley faces. Whenever her name popped up on my phone, or whenever I saw her at a party, I got a shot of adrenaline.

One day that spring, the "In a relationship" label disappeared from her Facebook profile. A few days later, on the last day of final exams, I suggested we get together.

She would be studying in Italy that summer. I would be studying in Spain.

"We could have our first date at some sandwich shop or whatever on campus. But supposedly, Venice is pretty romantic, what with the gondolas and all. And I'll only be a stone's throw away." (A line taken from Drew, a real ladies' man, during an impromptu pregame strategy session at the fraternity bathroom sinks.)

She smiled that knee-buckling smile of hers and said, "That sounds great."

A first date in *Venice*. Not even I could fuck that up.

CHAPTER 22

Mom's last words before I walked into the airport were, "Please, please do not run with the bulls."

In my head, I turned Mom into an enemy. I didn't tell her about road trips or spin-moves, just to feel like I was getting away with something. The truth is, she has supported — though surely worried about — everything I've ever done. Including spending that summer in Madrid. This was her one request.

"I won't, Mom," I said, as I closed the car door.

I ran with the bulls.

How could I not? The San Fermín Festival in Pamplona was a short bus ride away.

A million people packed the streets, decked out in white shirts and pants, most of which were stained red with sangria. The locals said the only people who run are dumb tourists. "It's dangerous, sometimes deadly, and what's even the point?" they asked. I told them I was young, fit, relatively sober, and wanted to feel alive.

There was no starting line, nor an announcement that it was time to get ready. Runners congregated at sunrise in the middle of a cobblestone street, which, after a light rain, was slippery. We were standing, waiting — for what I didn't know. I could feel my heart like footsteps in my chest. I kept shifting my weight and pulling my ankles behind my back to stretch.

Then, a loud crack, and everyone started running toward the bullring. I did, too. I felt like I was faster than most of the people around me. My strides were longer than they had ever been.

Another loud crack meant all the bulls were out of the pen. I knew looking over my shoulder would slow me down, but I did it anyway. Nothing there … yet.

After what seemed like a mile but was a quarter at most, I heard the cowbells around the bulls' necks. I turned and saw their horns and their rippling chest muscles and sheer mass. They were catching up quick.

I ducked into a doorway on the left, shoved my back against the door, and sucked in my stomach. Ten feet behind me, in the middle of the street, a man was a step ahead of the first bull. Then, the bull's front legs hit the man's calves and took him down, his belly smacking the cobblestone and his head barely missing it, an inch away from a concussion, or worse.

The bull kept running like it had stepped on a pebble. The man covered his head with his hands as the rest of the bulls, and all the people, ran ahead as if he weren't even there. Eventually, he stood up and, without dusting himself off, started running again toward the bullring.

CHAPTER 23

Cecilia and I arranged to meet on Venice's landmark Rialto Bridge on a Tuesday night in July.

On a gondola in the Grand Canal, I would quote *Doctor Faustus*. "O, thou art fairer than the evening air; clad in the beauty of a thousand stars; brighter art thou than flaming Jupiter; more lovely than the monarch of the sky."

Then I'd lean in and kiss her.

Obviously, girls wanted to be serenaded by a Romeo whose passion for them drove him to think up sweet, articulate words. Then, they wanted to ride off into the sunset.

What the fuck was I thinking? That's what they want *in sitcoms*.

I (barely) slept the previous night in the Zurich airport, waiting for my connecting flight to Venice. When I checked into my Venice hotel room — which I made sure had a view of the Canal, in case the night ended there — I tried to nap but couldn't fall asleep. I watched the hotel's one English language channel for hours, with the volume low, while pacing around the room, rehearsing my lines.

I went to the bridge, worrying she would stand me up — until I saw her through a crowd of people. I walked up to her and said with a smile, "Excuse me, Miss. I'm supposed to be meeting someone on the Rialto Bridge. Do you know where that might be?" (Another practiced line.)

She laughed and we clicked into our typical, flirty banter. We ate dinner, and when the bill came, she said, "We'll split it?"

"Don't even think about it." I was still stuck in the 1950s — or earlier. *Doctor Faustus* was written in the damn 1580s.

We wandered the city, just talking. I reached out my hand and said something dumb like, "There's this song that goes, 'I want to hold your hand.'"

It started raining, but she said she loved the rain.

"Um, you're wearing sandals," I said.

"So I'll be tough for a night."

She was perfect. I decided to love the rain, too.

The rain cleared the canal of gondolas and emptied the streets of pedestrians. The Sun set, the Moon rose, and we wound up back on the Rialto Bridge. I had sworn, while pacing in my hotel room, to stay within myself during that first kiss — not to get sped up and make mistakes like a point guard versus a full-court press. I wanted to remember it forever.

But the closest I can get to a memory of that moment

is the position of our bodies — her back was against the bridge's railing when we kissed, and then she turned around and faced the canal as I stood with my arms around her waist and my head over her right shoulder. We watched the lights and their reflection in the water, and heard the clapping of the waves against boats as they docked.

We were silent for a second. "I was hoping to catch you off-guard, but I guess I telegraphed it." She didn't immediately understand what I meant — she hadn't been hearing sports announcers describe interceptions since birth — but she smiled and said, "It was perfect."

We found the only gelato shop still open and sat against a brick wall under an awning to eat. She leaned over and rested her head on my shoulder. I put my arm around her and hoped she wouldn't be able to feel my heartbeat, or read my mind, in which I was screaming my voice hoarse and doing fist pumps like Tiger when he sank that putt to send the '08 U.S. Open into a playoff.

We stopped and kissed on every bridge we crossed. (Venice has more than 400 of them.) When we got to her visiting family's hotel, we kissed one last time. "I'll talk to you soon," I said, looking into her eyes with a sly smile. I knew she loved when I did that.

I floated through the empty streets, my eyes still seeing her bright blue ones looking up at me like I was the only thing in her world. I pored over every detail of the night: the tenderness of her lips; the smoothness of her hand as I held it; her laugh and her smile and her toughness. I started planning our second date: a candlelit slow dance in my fraternity room. James Taylor, whose concert in

Venice had been rained out that night, would be playing softly on my record player, singing, "There's something in the way she moves."

Did the thought occur to me of how I might propose, many years in the future, at midnight on the Golden Gate Bridge, because a bridge, like a marriage, joins two things as one? Nope, no way, not even for a second.

I'd decided not to ask her back to my hotel. I wanted to be a gentleman; there would be plenty of time for sex, and soon, I would be everything I wanted to be. The guy who goes all-in and over the top in everything, and makes it work. The guy who has it all.

CHAPTER 24

WIMBLEDON LADIES' SINGLES — FINAL:

KVITOVÁ VS. SHARAPOVA

LONDON, ENGLAND

July 2, 2011

I flew to London for the second weekend of
Wimbledon. I had a ticket for the plane. I did not have a
ticket for the tennis.

Early Saturday morning, I bussed to *Abbey Road* and
walked the famous crosswalk, deep in thought. I paused
in front of the studio where the Beatles recorded most of
their music. With tears in my eyes, I looked at the colorful graffiti on the white, brick walls. *Always in Revolution*;
We love you, yeah, yeah, yeah.

Dad spoke nervously about almost everything — his
job, his finances, his abilities as a father — but when he

spoke about the Beatles, his voice never wavered. They had been the soundtrack to those cozy bachelor weekends at his apartment, the one thing he loved that never let him down.

Once, at an elementary school festival, he saw my third-grade teacher in the crowded gym. I had told Dad that Mr. Stroud was a Beatles fan, too.

"Mr. Stroud — Let's see if you agree with me and Trev," Dad called out. "Best album: *Rubber Soul* or *Abbey Road*?"

"Hmm," Mr. Stroud said. "Gotta go with *Abbey Road*."

Dad jumped and ran a lap around the gym, pumping his arms over his head, shouting, "Wooo-hooo-hooo ... best album of all time, baby!"

The Gentlemen's Final at Wimbledon was on Sunday. My flight home was that evening, so I would've needed to bring all my belongings to the match. Bulky pockets would've hindered my stride, and a backpack would've been a major annoyance,[11] so I decided to spin the Ladies' Final on Saturday.

I tried to convince a fellow traveler to come with me.

"How're you getting tickets?" he asked.

"I'll probably just hop a fence or something," I said as casually as I could. The spin-move seemed cooler if people thought it was no big deal to me.

"I'm not hopping any fences, man," he smirked. "You're insane." I thought *he* was the insane one — unwilling to even scout perhaps his one chance to see a Wimbledon Final.

---

11   The less you carry, the better. Ideally: wallet, keys, phone.

I arrived thirty minutes before the start of the 2:00
p.m. match. The first step of a spin-move is to survey
everything.[12] At the All-England Club, I wandered
down the golf course fairways, from which I could see
the entrance to the tennis facility. It was behind a wire
fence — and a guard's booth.

I crept around the booth, which turned out to be
empty. I approached the fence. The bottom had begun
to curl upward. I got on all fours, then dropped my torso
to the ground and army-crawled under it.

I stood up, dusted off, and crossed the street. I saw
a path toward the tennis complex, but it was guarded
by a fence too tall to climb. Fences, of course, separate
people with access (tickets) from people without it. I
looked through and saw nothing more than fans walking
toward the tennis complex.

I kept walking. After maybe 20 steps, I noticed a door
handle. The fence had a gate.

In the movies, the door opens, the protagonist looks
over both shoulders as if he's confused, but no one's there,
so he shrugs and walks in. I turned the door handle and
pulled. It opened. I skipped the shrug; I knew exactly
what I was doing.

The gate opened to a sidewalk, which led to ...
the box office?

---

12   You can wander around aimlessly, while keeping an eye on doors, security
      guards, and crowd flow. Even if you stumble into a restricted area — may-
      be a media entrance or a construction zone — if you pretend to be lost
      and oblivious, security should give you the benefit of the doubt. You're not
      doing anything wrong until you actually enter a stadium without a ticket.
      Short of entering, go everywhere you can and check every door and win-
      dow. Arenas, stadiums, and tennis centers have so many doors that, odds
      are, one will be unlocked.

Now I was confused. I asked the attendant how much tickets cost.

"Obviously, stadium seats are sold out. But you can buy a ticket to watch the telly on the hill for 15 pounds." I paid and advanced to the next level of my mission.

Everyone was walking toward Henman Hill on the right. But when I looked left, maybe 50 feet away ... wasn't that the stadium? Above a garage-looking entryway, wide enough for eight cars, was a white sign that might as well have been a neon arrow pointing me toward the entrance below. The massive black letters read: *Centre Court.*

I walked closer. The entrance led to the underbelly of the stadium. Inside was a staircase.

I stood there as the other patrons filed toward the hill. Did they not notice? There was no fence, no door, no security guard, no usher, no cop — nothing between that staircase and me.

I walked right in. I took the staircase as high as it went.

On the stadium's upper concourse, I saw fans lined up to enter the seating sections. Two ushers, dressed in white, button-down smocks; white, perfectly ironed pants; and goofy constable hats with the brims pulled down over their eyes, checked tickets at each section. I had no chance there.

The match was about to begin. I had to find somewhere to watch. I opened an unmarked sliding door. I looked out, beyond a railing, and saw bright green grass and brilliant white chalk lines.

Two women in wheelchairs sat to my left. I had walked into an accessible-seating area.

"How's it going, I hope you don't mind if I join you here." They didn't. "It's just that I'm a huge Maria Sharapova fan and I get nervous when she plays, so I'd rather stand," I lied.

They invited me to stand behind them for the match. I would have preferred an area with more running room and an easier exit, but spin-movers can't be choosers. I had a clear view of the court, and nothing else mattered.[13]

I kept looking over my shoulder, hoping the sliding door behind me would stay closed. Eventually, it opened: two guys, about my age, in regular street clothes. I made room and introduced myself.

"What brings you guys up here?" I asked.

"Ah, we're on our break from Group 4," one of them said. I didn't want to be asked the same question, so I just nodded.

Then, a uniformed police officer opened the door and stood next to us. Shit. Of all the places he could've wandered into.

Go big or go home, Trev.

I tried to befriend him. "What a backhand, eh?" I commented. "Think Maria can overcome this?" He gave one-syllable answers to all my questions.

When the other guys left, presumably to go back to their duties with Group 4 (whatever that was), I said, "See ya guys later," and stayed put.

---

13   Once I'm inside an arena, I can contort myself however I need to, as long as I can see the game or match. Many gatecrashers take pride in sneaking into the first row, or into the locker room. To me, there's nobility in being a fan, in the upper deck, and sharing the experience with 20,000 other people. I've never really wanted to be courtside, on the bench, or in the home team's huddle. Besides, the closer you try to get to the action, the greater your chances of being asked to show a ticket.

"How'd you end up here?" the cop asked after a while, but he supplied an answer before I could respond. "You with Group 4?" [14]

"Yup," I said, and kept my focus on the match.

Petra Kvitová won the first set and was cruising in the second. During a changeover, the officer, suddenly perplexed, turned to me. "Hey ... how come you're not back at work?"

Uh-oh.

"The fellas know I'm a huge Sharapova fan, so they wanted me to be able to watch."

He was blocking my only escape. What would happen if I got arrested in another country?

"Let me see your pass," he demanded.

"Oh, I left it down there."

"You're not really with Group 4, are you?"

He was friendly, but he wasn't stupid.

"No." [15]

I stared at the ground, trying to look ashamed. Would I go to jail? Get deported? Did I know any immigration lawyers?

His expression turned stiff. I looked him in the eye. He held my life in his hands.

"Out." He pointed to the door. "Nicely tried." He slid the door open, pointed me out, and once more I

---

14   Authority figures are excellent, without realizing it, at providing the answers you need. Be patient when talking to them, and reveal as little information as possible.

15   Don't admit guilt until you've exhausted every other possible excuse. But once you've tried everything, don't insult your questioner's intelligence. Own up to it and hope for mercy.

considered running. "We're going downtown, chap," I imagined him saying.

I looked behind me. He closed the door. He was staying to watch the match! I hurried down a flight of stairs to the lower level of the stadium. I needed to get away from that officer, but I had never left a sporting event before it ended, and I had quietly cursed too many people who did, to start now.

I lucked out: With the match almost over, the ushers didn't mind if I stood next to them to watch. Kvitová won. Patrons filed out, creating the right diversion for me to slip past the ushers and into the front row to watch the trophy presentation.

Later, I couldn't help Googling "Group 4." It's the world's largest security company and has provided security at Wimbledon for years. Being mistaken for a security agent was the very thing that enabled me to (temporarily) dupe security.

be tempted to reach out again. But when my phone rang three days later, I recognized the area code. Al and Jim were in the room, so I told them, "This is an important call." I was hoping they would stick around for moral support. But as the phone rang a second time, they stood up. They were out the door by the third ring.

"Hi! How's it going?" I said when I answered.

"Oh, not bad. I spilled wine on my phone ... it's been broken the past couple days."

I thought about asking, "Is that the truth, or are you trying to let me down easy?" But I was afraid of the answer.

"Oh, gotcha. Well, I was just wondering if you might wanna hang out this week."

"Trevor, I've been thinking."

This cannot be happening.

"I don't want to pursue a relationship right now."

Down 4-3. Someone, please, call timeout.

I was in a trance. I said something pathetic like, "We can still be friends." I thanked her for being honest.

"You ... you make me feel good about myself," I stuttered.

"Good. I like to make people feel good."

5-3. The insult-to-injury dagger into the empty net. That was the best she could come up with? Not even an apology?

I said goodbye and tossed my phone onto the coffee table. If I couldn't find a girlfriend in fucking college, how would I ever do it?

I stared blankly at the white cinder block wall of my room — the clock-winding-down-with-your-team-way-behind stare — and into my miserable destiny.

I was looking out the window of an adult day care, scraggly-bearded, in pajamas, sedated by a cocktail of prescription drugs, obsessing over the wreckage of my once-bright future.

At least my father had a son to sometimes answer his calls. I wouldn't even have that.

CHAPTER 26

"Today is the day we've been waiting our whole lives for," I wrote on my fantasy football message board in the wee hours of the morning. "All the losses, all the suffering ... it all led to this."

It was October 27, 2006. I was a sophomore in high school.

If North American sports awarded championships to the best team over the course of the season, like European soccer, the Cardinals would have won titles in 2004 and 2005. Instead, championships go to the winners of crapshoot playoff tournaments. The playoffs are exciting, obviously, but sports are pretty random in such small sample sizes. All that franchises can do is consistently make the playoffs to give themselves more spins at the roulette wheel.

The Cardinals were mediocre during that regular season but squeaked into the playoffs — and were leading the World Series three games to one.

When Dad walked in the front door, he said, "I'm so jealous. Tonight, you get to win your first World Series."

Connor, Dad, and I watched in the basement, while Mom and her mom watched upstairs. Neither Mom nor Grandma liked watching games with Dad. His face turned too red, he paced too much, and by the seventh inning, he would already have said, more than a dozen times, "You guys, I can't believe they didn't score in the second. This game would be over!"

But heading into the ninth, with the Cardinals leading, the parties merged in the living room.

"Congratulations, fellas," Dad said. "Just in case we get too excited, I wanted to tell you that now."

"Don't say that, Bryan!" Grandma snapped. "It's not over yet." Dad looked at me and Connor with a smile that said it was. The guy who usually saw nothing but pitfalls now saw a sure thing.

Mom and Grandma were sitting on the couch; the Three Kraus Men were standing, Dad between his two sons, his arms around our shoulders. He leaned down to put his mouth to our ears. "Congratulations, guys," he whispered.

I know Adam Wainwright struck out Brandon Inge. I've seen the replay hundreds of times. I'm sure we all jumped and hugged and high-fived and screamed.

I know the next day's newspaper headline was, simply, "YES!" Dad called me and said, "At first, I didn't know how I felt about that headline … but then, throughout the day, I found myself throwing my arms up and saying, 'YES!'"

But the truth is, I don't remember that final out.

defensive backfield over beers, you can *feel* the game on people's minds. They're celebrating tonight because tomorrow is going to be a great day. Tomorrow is going to be a great day because there's a tailgate, then a game. Tomorrow night's plans — a party for a win, a pity-party for a loss — depend on the game's outcome. Either way, for 24 hours, the game dominates the lives of a few hundred thousand people.

I remember passing a college-aged girl on the sidewalk who had just turned away from a loud argument with her boyfriend. An older woman in a red-and-white-checkered shirt walked past her and said, "It'll be ok, honey. Roll Tide."

With tears streaming down her cheeks, she took a deep breath through her snot-congested nose, looked at the woman, and said, "Roll Tide."

My plan usually was to get tipsy the night before a big game, but not too tipsy, because I had to wake up in a few hours to tailgate and drink more. But on our trip to Tuscaloosa, we were nervous. The next day, we would be busting five people into The Game of the Century. So we got hammered.

At one bar, my friends' fake IDs worked. Mine said I was Trevor Pryce (former Broncos defensive end; first name that came to mind when I bought it) and listed an address in Calgary, Alberta. Unfortunately, it was in an evidence room in the Columbia, MO police station.

A few months earlier, the cops had stormed into a bar I was at. The officer's statement, which I obtained in court, reads: "We entered the establishment and Officer Clements located two subjects that appeared to be underage. Officer Clements made contact with one subject, and the other subject, later identified as Trevor Kraus, began to briskly walk. I advised Kraus to stop but he continued through the crowd. I recontacted Kraus on the dance floor area of the business and observed him with a Bud Light beer bottle in his hand. I asked Kraus why he continued to walk away from me after I had told him to stop and he advised because he was 19 years old. Kraus was escorted out of the business."

At the bar in Tuscaloosa, I went around to the side of the patio, which was guarded by a short, white picket fence. I stepped over it, but my foot landed on a stack of cardboard boxes. I lost my balance and fell into a table, scattering condiments all over the floor.

Two bouncers grabbed me and took me outside the front entrance. One of the bouncers said to the other, "Hold onto him until the Big Bad Wolf gets here."

I did not want to find out who the Big Bad Wolf was. As soon as the bouncer's grip on my shoulder loosened, I took off running into the crowded street and got away.

The next morning, a TV reporter was looking to interview people who had traveled long distances to see the game. I volunteered. Before starting to record, she asked how we got tickets.

"We don't exactly have tickets."

"Oh. How are you gonna get them?"

"We'll figure something out," I winked to my friends.

Two hours before kickoff, we swapped our preppy tailgate attire for spin-move gear: hats, jackets, red undershirts, and running shoes. We paced the exterior of Bryant-Denny Stadium.

"Alright, I like the setup at these three. I'll take Gate 37. Al, you're on 38. Drew, you've got 39," I said. "Jim, Ben — you remember that entrance on the other side, with the stairs behind the ticket takers? I think that's your best bet."

Before we split, we agreed to meet in Section GG at kickoff. I was clear: If someone got caught, we would deal with it after the game.[20] But I couldn't help thinking my friends' spin-moves were on me. What if they tripped on their way in and were hauled to jail?

I had never watched someone else spin, and seeing a friend pull it off … observing the ticket takers' confusion, watching them contemplate chasing before giving up … would be one of the coolest moments of my life. The spin-move was my baby — and I had inspired others to follow. I couldn't be crazy. Followers are the difference between legend and lunatic.

But my line moved quickest, so I became the lead-off hitter. My ticket taker stood two steps in front of a 10-foot-wide opening that led into the stadium. There were no turnstiles.

I walked toward her, and when she reached for my ticket, I sprinted past.

I spotted a ramp to the right and kept running until I reached the top. I looked behind me as I changed clothes. Security had no chance. I walked to the nearest

---

20   If you're going for a multi-person spin and you get caught, any security guard or supervisor worth a damn will ask, "You're with those other guys, right?" You have to swear you don't know them, and be willing to endure any and all punishment alone. If you make it in safely but your friend(s) get caught, enjoy the game, *leave the stadium* afterward, and pretend you hadn't been inside when you show up to bail your buddies out.

concession stand with long strides and heavy breaths. I bought a bag of peanuts, then headed to Section GG.

A few minutes passed, and I began to eat my peanuts. I struggled to crack the shells — my hands were trembling with adrenaline and fear for my friends. All I could think about were untied shoelaces and handcuffs. I tried to focus on the simple routine. Crack the shell, pop the peanuts in my mouth, toss the shell on the ground.

I had almost finished the bag when I saw Al's goofy grin appear from around a corner. I skipped over to him, cackling like a hyena, and hugged him.

"Talk to me."

He exhaled. "I was so nervous, man. But I kept thinking about how much it would suck to be the one guy who didn't make it. Otherwise, I don't know if I could've done it."

"Nothin' like the nerves of that first spin."

"They saw you go and they all kinda stood up straighter, so I got out of line and took another lap. Halfway around, I saw a ticket taker who was chatting away with someone and she was standing way in front of the gate. So I came in from the side, sort of speed-walking, got past her, and took off."

We felt taps on our shoulders. It was Drew.

He had a few petty crimes in his past and was a born schemer, so I thought he would be cool and calm. But he had been the most nervous among us, spending the afternoon self-medicating with cigarettes and beer.[21]

---

21   I prefer to spin sober; I want a clear mind and smooth motor skills. Besides, the rush of it is better than any liquor or drug I know. But there are no pictures on the scorecard. Do what you gotta do.

Saturday, Nov. 5 marked another successful security breach for the infamous Trevor Kraus. Armed with cool confidence and a sack of steel, the junior led a gang of goons past unsuspecting ushers and into the high-profile Alabama vs. LSU game. Who needs turnstiles when you know how to turn with style? The break-in extended Kraus's streak of unpaid-for sporting events to seven, including World Series Games 2, 4, and 7, last year's Mizzou-kU basketball game, and a Wimbledon Final. So what's next for the Sultan of Spin? The possibilities are endless:

6. The Super Bowl – *He might have done it at the World Series, but the Super Bowl is a different story. Presidential and celebrity appearances tend to be more frequent, and eyes are everywhere. He'll need the full arsenal of Madden maneuvers (the juke, the stiff-arm, the dive, and yes, the spin).*

5. An Airplane – *Dodging 80-year-old, half-blind ushers at sporting events gets boring. The real question is whether the swift-thinking Kraus is daring enough to take on airport security. Bypassing both the security checkpoint and the gate will be tough without a boarding pass, but this kid is unreal with adrenaline and a splash of madness coursing through his veins. Plus, who doesn't want to see a lanky kid in a Blues jersey chased by some 250-pound woman in a TSA uniform?*

4. Area 51 – *There are signs outside this government-protected territory that say, "Use of deadly force is authorized." We don't think that will deter the brave Trevor Kraus, who could become the CIA's top stealth-operation spy if he can sneak into this mysterious military base. If he doesn't make it back, at least we can look forward to conspiracy theories about his frozen body being sacrificed to appease carnivorous extraterrestrials.*

3. The White House – *The chances of our resident journalist duping Secret Service are slim to none, but I'd love to be a fly on*

*the wall when this plan hits the drawing board. Mix in a little
National Treasure with a splash of Ocean's Eleven and steal
some trade secrets from Tom Clancy's book-turned-video game
Splinter Cell, and he'll have it: a foolproof plan to spin-move
the Presidential Palace.*

2. North Korea *– You have to infiltrate Kim Jong-il's domain
of doom to be considered a true badass. All that money saved on
college football games will subsidize airfare to Seoul (unless he
spin-moves the plane), but crossing the perilous Demilitarized
Zone could get sticky.*

1. Vagina *– The man isn't exactly a rat-slaying fratstar. At
the rate he's going, no one really knows if he'll be able to slide in
there without paying. Ironically, this is the only scenario where
buying a ticket is illegal.*

Most of us talked that way about women. Some did it
to sound cool; others truly believed women were sexual
objects. I knew it was terrible, but if you'd caught me in
an honest moment — drunk at a party, standing alone in
the corner, trying to think of some formula of words to say
to some pretty girl on the dance floor — well, I don't think
I ever would have said I wanted to "slay rats." But I wanted
to *want* to be the kind of guy who did.

I had to remove myself from the fraternity — either
emotionally, by writing the newsletter, or physically, by
taking road trips — to realize that I was every bit as sexist
as Those Guys. I didn't think of girls (I wish I would have
thought of them as *women* — that would have been a good
start) as sexual objects, but I did see them as sounding
boards to confirm my "brilliance." As trophies to show off.

"To slay rats" was part of the house's dialect, so I left that term in. But I cut a sentence from the last paragraph: "There's some speculation as to whether or not he's a virgin." Once a semester, the fraternity gathered in a circle for a bonding activity with the pledges called "Step Out." As a freshman, I told everyone, openly and honestly, about my first kiss. As a sophomore, when the command came to "step to the center if you're a virgin," I hesitated for a second, then gritted my teeth and stepped forward.

But as a junior — an upperclassman! — I looked at those freshmen pledges and couldn't get the lyrics to Kid Rock's "All Summer Long" out of my head. I assumed they all were coming off idyllic summers of "sipping whiskey out the bottle" and "making love out by the lake to [a] favorite song."

When I thought about how far behind I was in the sex game, the girlfriend game, the happiness game, I wanted to bite down on cold steel and lobotomize the part of my brain that knew the truth with a bullet.

I knew sex shouldn't have been currency, but the fraternity was a competition. The winners were those who got drunk all the time and got laid every weekend — at the library, on the quad, or on the 50-yard line at the football stadium — without even trying and still had their lives together enough to do well in school, work out, and be involved in campus organizations. The guys who had it all.

It was Those Guys who would ask me, as I was heading to a regular season Mizzou basketball game against Texas Tech in a half-empty arena on a Tuesday night in January, "Ooh, are you spinning?"

Of course not. I didn't spin ordinary games because that would diminish the thrill when it mattered.

In 2005, I started saving my ticket stubs. As I write this in 2018, my scrapbook contains 580 used tickets to sporting events. Including the events I worked during my four years as an usher, that's more than one game legally attended per week. I've spin-moved just 31 (plus, yeah, a few movies, museums, and coffee shop bathrooms without buying coffee).[24]

But a fraternity is no place for philosophy. When the virgin question came this time during "Step Out" — when the moment arrived for me to admit that I didn't have it all, that wanting it badly enough didn't work, and that there was a glaring hole in my résumé as a man — my cheeks flushed with embarrassment, and I glued my feet to the floor.

---

24   These nine spin-moves were omitted from the narrative of *Ticketless*:

Missouri vs. Illinois, December 22, 2010; Chicago at St. Louis Blues, December 28, 2010; Chicago at St. Louis Blues, December 3, 2011; kansas at Missouri, February 4, 2012; Florida at Missouri, October 19, 2013; Mets at Cardinals, July 19, 2015; Buccaneers at Rams, December 17, 2015; Santa Clara at San Francisco, February 9, 2017; Getafe at Leganés, December 7, 2018.

I describe the Bucs-Rams spin-move on page 335 in the "Extra Innings" section. If you're interested in reading about the other eight, email me with the subject line "SPIN-MOVES" at: trevor@ticketless.pub.

CHAPTER 29

The Super Bowl is usually in warm-weather cities. During my junior year, however, it was in Indianapolis, just six hours east on Highway 70.

Security would be outrageous; the CIA, FBI, NSA, and Secret Service would all be there. I heard rumors of an armed helicopter circling the stadium.

But security and metal detectors would likely be in front of the ticket takers. That's the key to the spin-move. Theoretically, I could run past a ticket taker without causing alarm because I would already have been through security, like all the other fans in the stadium. In practice, however, I doubted some FBI agent would see me running at full speed and think, "Ah, he's no threat, he already made it through the metal detectors." I needed an alternative to the traditional spin-move.

Super Bowl ticketholders often insert their tickets into plastic sleeves attached to neck lanyards for safekeeping.

If I had a ticket in a lanyard, no one would touch it or see it up close.

I did some Googling and found a picture of a woman with spiked hair and glasses, holding two tickets in her hand. The tickets were for Section 422, Row 14, and the Super Bowl XLVI logo made a half-circle around the top of the Lombardi Trophy. Face value was $900.

Now that I look it up, Indiana law distinguishes petty theft (goods of less than $500) from grand theft, which is a felony. But I wasn't "stealing" because I wouldn't profit like the counterfeiters I read about online. Besides, I figured (wrongly, as I almost learned the hard way) the only victim of my forgery would be the corrupt, multi-billion-dollar cartel called the National Football League.[25]

My Photoshop skills weren't good enough to align and enlarge the ticket without damaging the quality of the image. But Michelle's were. She had been a teaching assistant in my computer design class the previous semester.

On the first day of that class, within four seconds of walking in late, I noticed, in this order: her pretty face, her long, brown hair, her massive breasts, her enthusiasm for her craft, and the self-confidence in her speech. She seemed like the kind of person who was bubbly and happy all the time, and goddamn, wasn't that exactly what I needed to balance out my always-serious intensity?

I played the class clown that first day, cracking jokes about how bad I was at "computer stuff." I stayed behind after class, pretending to fumble my papers into my

---

25   I'm not an attorney, obviously. But in Chapter 66, I argue that spin-moving falls into a legal vacuum, wherein the supposed victims don't really lose anything.

backpack. Once the room was empty, I said, "Hey, question. So you're a T.A. Does that make you technically a teacher or a student?"

"I'm definitely a student," she said.

I exaggerated a sigh of relief. "Phew. Guess I won't violate any regulations by asking you out, then."

She tilted her head slightly and flashed a smile, as if to consider it, for half a heartbeat. Then she chuckled, "Wow, that was pretty ballsy. But I have a boyfriend."

I had to keep a poker face while cursing under my breath. "Lucky guy," I said.

We walked out of the building together, grasping for another topic of conversation. She turned left, and although I was also headed left, I went right, waved goodbye, and kicked a pebble down the sidewalk for a while before turning around.

I flirted with her the rest of the semester, but we fell out of touch when the course ended.

The week of the Super Bowl, I reached out to her. We met in one of the journalism buildings, and I showed her the picture. In three minutes, she cropped a perfectly sized, upright, high-resolution image of a ticket to Super Bowl XLVI.

Every so often, she looked at me and shook her head, like she could see right through my attempt to impress her. While she put the finishing touches on the image, she happened to mention, oh so casually, that she had broken up with her boyfriend.

She was right: The fake ticket was, partly, an attempt to impress her. But I also intended to use it.

CHAPTER 30

Dad made it clear: We weren't rooting for people to die. We were "only" rooting for billions of dollars in damage to buildings and homes.

We were diehard hurricane fans. August and September, when ocean waters are warmest, were our playoffs. The Weather Channel was our ESPN. Dad's world atlas, where we tracked storm coordinates, was our sports page.

Hurricanes weakened, strengthened, and wobbled from their trajectories like teams won and lost, and Dad would sit in his recliner, mesmerized by the TV, running his fingernails along his palms, enjoying the drama. So I did the same.

"Nothing's more entertaining than a major hurricane bearing down on a major city," he said. Panic and chaos made for good TV, and Dad loved good TV — whether it was the NCAA Tournament or a steep drop in the stock market.

Because he had never steered us wrong — whether escorting us into Wrigley Field, criticizing La Russa's lineup decisions, or explaining the perfection of the cheese-to-sauce ratio at some pizza parlor across town — I took what he said as fact.

We knew that New Orleans lies at the bottom of a basin, surrounded by the Gulf of Mexico, Lake Pontchartrain, and the Mississippi River — and what that might mean if a hurricane struck — before most people realized. We knew a Category 5 hurricane hitting New Orleans would be the most dramatic storyline in the country for months. And we wanted it. Bad.

One hurricane season, we got our wish: Katrina.

Dad, I'm sure, would say our rooting had no effect. He would be right. He would probably say, "Look at how we consume the news: We read newspapers as a way to entertain ourselves while riding trains or eating cereal. Look at how TV stations play their dramatic BREAKING NEWS theme songs as they come back from commercial to announce something terrible. They present it as theater: protagonists, villains, plot twists, and all. Try to tell me coverage of Democrats vs. Republicans doesn't remind you of Red Sox vs. Yankees."

He would, once again, be right.

But thousands of people died. Millions of people suffered. We had rooted for it. We had rooted for it to hit at high tide.

As we watched the terror, the flooding, the chaos, and the death, I knew, for the first time, my dad was wrong.

CHAPTER 31

On September 3, 2011, I wrote in my journal about asking Michelle out. "Have I rebounded from Cecilia? No. A sick, perverse part of me still thinks there's a chance with her."

That same entry said: "Jim and Al are currently in the room, giving me shit for writing this journal. 'Nobody wants to read about you brushing your teeth and wiping your ass,' they said. What do they want me to write about? Do they want me to write about the gut-wrenching mood swings I've been going through since I got back from Europe? Do they want me to write about how I feel completely alone at times, but other times, I feel like I have the greatest friends in the world? Do they want me to write about how, when everyone around me is partying or seems to be having fun, I want to blow my brains out?"

I thought about killing myself — every day, multiple times a day, for hundreds of days in a row.

I was never actually going to doing it. I could always tell myself, *Stop it, Trevor. This is pathetic. Rub some dirt on it. Get it together. Tough it out. Grit your teeth. Play through the pain. Make it work.*

But I had my own funeral music planned out: The dark version of the James Bond theme song that the *Goldeneye* video game played when your character was killed, followed by the "St. Louis Blues," the W.C. Handy song from which the team took its name. The organist plays it after losses, to make sure they sink in.

I was certain I'd be alone forever. Sports fandom had infected my mind, as it did to Dad's. Like him, I would burn out.

Whether it's the sports ethos of aggression and intensity, the brain chemistry I inherited from him, or both, I've always believed that if you want the payoff — the championship; the relationship — to mean as much as it possibly can, you have to go all-in, all the time. It's why Dad said we had to be "true fans." But when you go all-in on something, you also give it the power to cripple you.

I thought I had to respond to every emotion with the absolute strongest, most intense reaction. When I liked a hockey team, I watched every second of every game. When I liked a girl, I took her on a first date in Venice. And the strongest reaction to my hopelessness was biting a pistol and firing a bullet through my skull.

Mom once showed me a story that Pop, my dad's dad, wrote for her. It was dated December, 1995 and began, "In pondering the purpose of our being, at least one

answer makes some sense to me: Try to find meaning in
the 'little moments' of life."

Pop described seeing 18-month-old Connor chasing
me, almost five years old, around his house. He told me
to stop running and to ask Connor why he was chasing.

"Trevor apparently agrees and suddenly stops, stat-
ue-like, his face in mock-frightened tension as Connor
approaches. And what does Connor do? He puts his
arms around his brother in a monster hug, as if to lift
him. And Trevor hugs his little brother back. They face
me, in a pose I want to freeze and frame: the boys em-
braced forever in childhood innocence and love."

"I know the scene cannot be seized and held. Nor
could any photograph convey the moment. And as I
look, I am already nostalgic for that moment's singular splendor."

Pop wrote that in those moments — in which you're
absorbed, fulfilled, and engaged; emotional, happy, and
in awe — "any questions of existence seem absurd."

My grandpa found such a moment in a hug between
his grandchildren. I find them in sports stadiums.

I know it sounds ridiculous, but thinking about my
brother, and how it would ruin the moment for him if
the Blues won the Stanley Cup and I wasn't there to hug
him, probably kept me from actually considering suicide.

Our one and only job, according to Dad, was to love
each other. "I'll die a happy man if I know you two are
the tightest pair of brothers in the whole wide world,"
he said when we would pose for a picture with our arms
around each other.

If I could bring him back for just 30 seconds, I would tell him that Connor saved my life; that he and I have become so close, we're extensions of each other. And that we have our daddy to thank.

While I might have been on my way to depression or insanity, it wasn't too late for Connor to strive for an even emotional keel. He could still turn out like Mom: levelheaded and able to roll with life's punches. I was the one who would become Dad, but I could pretend to be strong for Connor. Besides, he had heard the "St. Louis Blues" often enough.

I don't consider myself conniving, but I understand why others do. Give me "calculating" or "crafty," perhaps. Connor is more social and studious, and less competitive. He has earned his reputation as an honest, pleasant, and thoughtful guy in all of his social circles.

He wouldn't devise schemes and spin-moves. But he can be talked into them.

The Dark Knight Batman movie premiered at midnight on July 18, 2008, shortly after I got my first car, the '99 Maxima I still drive. We could have told Mom we wanted to go to the movie, and she probably would have let us, but it would be more fun without permission.

Our rooms were across from each other, at the end of a long, carpeted hallway. The staircase was at the other end, next to Mom's room. She was a light sleeper and slept with the door open.

That night, we went to bed early, as Mom's TV flickered. I closed my door from the outside — loudly, on purpose — so she would hear the click of the handle. I tiptoed into Connor's room.

"How do we do this?" he asked.

"Careful on the third step from the bottom — it's creaky. I already put our shoes at the front door. Once we get down there, we carry our shoes outside, close the door gently, and we're gone."

We crept with our backs against the walls of the hallway. Mom's bedroom had a full-length mirror that, if she happened to startle awake, would give her a view into the hallway. We went down the stairs in white socks, stepped over the third from the bottom, slipped out the door, and headed to the theater.

I'll never forget plopping into our movie theater seats, safe and sound, Mom none the wiser, as the crowd buzzed with the same eager energy that bounces off the walls of a football stadium just before kickoff.

I don't remember a thing about the movie.

CHAPTER 32

I bought thick, glossy paper at an office supply store, and handed a flash drive to the woman at the desk. She loaded my "ticket" on her computer and raised her eyebrows. Did she realize I was creating a $900 counterfeit?

"My brother is a big football fan … his birthday is tonight, so I'm gonna play a little prank on him," I chuckled.

She shrugged and printed two color copies. The second was for Cody, a former high school offensive tackle who adored the game of football — and the institution of the Super Bowl — on a level no one else in the fraternity, myself included, could match.

Cody called me at two in the morning, a few hours before we were supposed to leave, as I lay staring at the ceiling. He was backing out.

"What?!"

"I told my mom about the plan, and she said it wasn't such a good idea."

It amazed me how obedient my college peers could

be to their parents. Once you reach a certain age (for me, about 12, when I started ignoring my mom's pleas to turn off the video games and get some sleep), parents' words morph from laws into suggestions.

Cody was testing my resolve. I think he wanted to know if I was sure we'd get in.

I had never been unsure of a spin-move. Nervous, yes, but I always knew I could outrun any cop. I wanted to say, "Of course we'll get in. Everything always works out."

But as much as I wanted to believe I could beat the cameras, and the guns, and the motion sensors, I knew I couldn't.

CHAPTER 33

January 21, 2012

Two weeks before the Super Bowl, I couldn't even beat a part-time security guard at my old stomping grounds.

Connor and I had tickets to a sold-out Blues-Sabres game in St. Louis, but Bruce, from Buffalo, wanted to see his hometown team as well. I gave him my ticket and told him to go inside and navigate to a set of exit-only doors across from Section 108. I had done the same thing a year earlier, with a different friend, before a game against Chicago. It had worked perfectly.

I went to those same doors and stood outside to wait for Bruce. He arrived soon after and opened them. I stepped inside. We turned to run up a nearby staircase, but a security guard was standing on the first step. He grabbed me by the shoulder.

I yelled at Bruce, "Run!" He could have eluded the guard's other hand and sprinted up the staircase. At least one of us would have made it. The guard said, "Stop right there." Bruce froze on the first step.[26]

The guard pushed open the door and shoved me out. He made Bruce surrender his ticket, then pushed him out, too. We crossed the street with our heads hanging.

"Dude, I'm so sorry," I said. "I want you to know: I'm downright ashamed of myself."

"Nah, don't worry about it, I agreed to do it. Let's just grab a couple tickets and enjoy the game."

The game began, the scalpers became desperate to unload their inventory, and they lowered their prices. We bought two standing-room-only tickets, but we sat in the row of our original tickets, next to Connor. It didn't cross my mind that we should have sat somewhere else — until I saw that same security guard climbing the steps toward our seats.

"We should be fine," I whispered to Bruce. "We have legitimate tickets. I guess he kept your previous ticket and decided to check this row? I don't get this."

"You're off your game, Trev."

The guard got to our seats and said to follow him. We did, into the concourse, where two additional guards

---

26   Bruce probably could've gotten away. Even if he had been caught, I think his offense would have been "trespassing," not "trespassing plus running away from security." I have to admit, though, I've always been afraid to look into what the charge would be for spin-moving. It probably varies from state to state, but trespassing, which is one of those misdemeanors a lawyer negotiates down to "loitering" or whatever, sounds about right.

and a supervisor surrounded us. They were taking us to the police room, which contained a small holding cell.

From the escalator, I could see the lower-level concourse. If we ran as soon as we hit the bottom, we could climb a small maintenance staircase that led to a door that would take us outside. But we hadn't done anything wrong — at least, not since we got busted the first time and were correspondingly punished.

We got to the police room. "Guys," I said before anyone else could speak, "I admit it: We tried to sneak in before. But then we bought legal tickets." I showed them to the supervisor, whom I recognized from when I worked there. He didn't seem to recognize me.

"You were told not to come back tonight," the supervisor said.

"No sir, that's not true. We were never told we couldn't come back."

Luckily, the original guard spoke up: "He's right. I said something like, 'Have a good night, guys.'"

"Alright. Well, look, here's the deal," the supervisor said. "Leave now, don't try to come back, and we won't get the cops involved."

Part of me was proud of my former coworkers. They were the first to thwart a spin-move. They had the doors covered, and they followed up by checking the seat on the confiscated ticket. They deserved more credit than I had given them.

But I sat quietly, with a scowl on my face, as Bruce and I watched the rest of the game at a bar across the street. I had let him down. I was pissed at myself. I had gotten careless. I didn't tell Bruce to look around before opening the door for me. I forgot the security guard had Bruce's ticket and would know to check that seat. I figured my knowledge of the arena would make it an easy spin, and I hadn't bothered to bring my A-Game.

Getting caught at a regular season hockey game by arena security was one thing. Getting caught at the Super Bowl by Homeland Security would be another.

CHAPTER 34

SUPER BOWL XLVI: GIANTS VS. PATRIOTS

INDIANAPOLIS, IN

February 5, 2012

"I can't make any guarantees," I told Cody. "We both know what we're up against. But what if, when we're 80, we've never been to a Super Bowl, and we turn on the game and think, *I wish I'd had the guts to go that one time in college.* Think about how much that would hurt."

There was a long silence.

"What happens if we get caught?"

"I don't know. But when we get there, if it doesn't look like it's gonna happen, we can drive right home."

"Alright, Trev. Let's do it."

Under the flickering light of my desk lamp, I made the final alterations to the "tickets." I used a glue stick to bond the glossy fakes to two Cardinals ticket stubs from the previous summer, which gave my forgeries proper thickness and fine print on the back, like real tickets. When the glue dried, I put my masterpieces in plastic cases that dangled from lanyards.

We hit the road early Sunday morning to arrive at the stadium in Indianapolis by the time the doors opened at 2:00 p.m., four and a half hours before kickoff. At most sporting events, security and metal detectors stand immediately inside the stadium. A little further inside are the ticket takers, and then you're on the concourse, looking for your section, row, and seat.

At the Super Bowl, there was a fenced perimeter a hundred yards from the stadium doors.

An article in the *Indianapolis Star* said that during Super Bowl weekend, the Indianapolis Police Department would disregard minor offenses, including trespassing, in exchange for a small contribution to a local charity. But the police's generosity probably didn't extend to trespassing *into the game.*

Fans waited in line before the gates even opened. They wore lanyards like ours. We approached the first entrance we saw, and I outlined the gameplan to Cody.

"The first line of defense is the metal detectors. Someone might glance at our tickets, but we'll keep moving."

There were eight metal detectors, lined side by side, spanning the width of the security tent.

"After that is where the work starts. Looks like there's room after the detectors, before the ticket takers, so that'll give us a chance to regroup."

Behind the ticket takers was a maze of fences that wound toward the stadium. "There could be one more checkpoint between the ticket takers and the stadium. But one game at a time," I said.

We put our phones and wallets in the little white boxes on the conveyor belt. Our lanyards stayed on our necks. We walked through a metal detector. The guard glanced at the tickets dangling near our stomachs, returned our wallets and phones, and motioned us onward.

As we moved toward the ticket takers, I leaned toward Cody.

"I'll go first. If, somehow, I get in and you don't, I'll find a way to get you in. It'll be easier from the inside. But if everything goes to hell, tell them you bought this ticket 30 minutes ago from a scalper, and you spent your life's savings on it. The more demonstrative you are, the more you push it, the more believable you'll be. You have to *demand* they let you in." [27]

I reached the front of my ticket line. The ticket taker, a woman, perhaps in her late 40s, cradled my lanyard in her left hand. She angled her scanner toward the lower barcode — the one from a Cardinals game six months earlier. She pressed 'Enter' on her scanner. It buzzed, and the screen displayed a red X.

"I'm sorry about this, sir. Do you mind taking your ticket out?"

As a matter of fact, I do.

She asked politely, but when you're up to no good, it

---

27   As Scott Kerman writes in *No Ticket, No Problem!*, "When dealing with stadium personnel, never entertain any suggestion that your story is question-
able. Always express shock if there is resistance."

feels like everyone is suspicious. My hands trembled as
I fumbled with my counterfeit. A trace amount of glue
had stuck to the lanyard, so I had to yank the ticket out.

I handed it to her. "Why don't you try the top barcode?" I squeaked.

She shook her head. "They're the same."

Another scan of the bottom barcode, another red X.

I scratched my head. "Wha … what's going on?"

"Just a moment, sir, let me get a supervisor.
Come with me."

She vacated her post and walked toward a table in the
middle of the tent. I had an open path to the fence maze
that led to the stadium. I took a deep breath. My calves
quivered. I was ready.

But I would be admitting guilt if I ran. The traditional spin-move would be an option later, at a different
entrance. Might as well see the ticket jig through.

I followed the ticket taker to a supervisor who sat at a
table in the middle of the security tent. He was in his 60s
or 70s and wore a black suit and earpiece.

"Ticket doesn't scan," the ticket taker said as she gave
it to him. She returned to her post. The supervisor stood,
seemingly a vertebra at a time. He took a scanner from
his pocket. I heard nothing except the sound of my heart
beating. I saw nothing except the image in my mind of
a cartoon character's heart throbbing so violently that it
bulges out of his chest.

I was in the middle of a security tent at the Super
Bowl. Every intelligence, defense, and security agency in
the country was there. I had a piece of paper from FedEx.

He scanned the bottom barcode. Another red X. He

let the scanner dangle from the Velcro attachment on his wrist as he examined the ticket. I had taken it out of the lanyard, the ticket taker had handled it, and now the supervisor was holding it. The glue had deteriorated, and the glossy printer paper was peeling away from the Cardinals ticket. The supervisor picked at a corner and peeled it further, until the picture of outfielder Matt Holiday swinging a bat was in plain sight. He stopped just short of peeling the whole thing apart.

It was over. There was no choice but to launch into the whole "I've been scammed" routine. I raised my eyebrows, puckered my lips, and thrust my jaw forward to look angry.

"Hmm, looks like your ticket got stuck to this old baseball ticket." Surprisingly, he sounded earnest.

"Huh." My voice cracked again. "I don't know how that would've happened. Maybe try scanning this other barcode."

The last syllable was barely out of my mouth when he flicked his wrist and readied his scanner. In slow motion, I saw him angle it toward the top barcode and press 'Enter.'

A beep, and a green checkmark.

"Oh. I'm, uh … hmm," he said. He regained his composure. "I'm sorry about that, sir. Happens all the time."

I had no idea what he was talking about. He handed me the ticket and I shoved it into the lanyard. He put his hand on my shoulder as we turned back toward the ticket taker. "He's good," he shouted to her. "Enjoy the game, sir."

Holy shit.

My legs carried me past the ticket taker. I didn't know what the hell was going on. I didn't care.

Holy shit!

I reached the maze of fences, turned a corner, and waited for Cody. I didn't dare return to the scene of the crime. I paced back and forth, hoping Cody would emerge.

I don't know how long I waited. Maybe a minute. The only thought I could process was: No Cody.

After another minute: Still, no Cody.

Finally, he strutted around the corner. I smiled and shook his hand. I mouthed, "Oh my god, oh my god, oh my god." I ached to know what happened. I waited to ask. We still weren't in the stadium.

We followed the fence maze toward it and saw the glass doors that opened into the concourse. One more hurdle: an usher standing to the right of those doors. With Cody behind me, I approached from the left.

We had not gone through all that, only to get stopped by this feeble last line of defense. He barked, "I need to check your tickets." I stayed as far away from him as I could, while still angling toward the door. I held up my lanyard, and Cody held up his. The usher gave thumbs up, and we walked into the Super Bowl.

I wish I could bottle that feeling and pour it on my cereal every morning.

After a full lap around the concourse, I felt safe. My ticket, though clearly fake, had scanned. Cody's had the same barcode and therefore should not have scanned.

"What exactly did we just pull off?" I asked. "What the hell happened back there?"

"Trev, it's the damndest thing," Cody said with wide eyes. "After you went in, I got to the ticket taker and that same supervisor came over and asked if I was with you."

"What did you say?"

"I said yeah. He tried scanning my ticket, it didn't work, and he peeled it apart. Then he said, 'You've been scammed, sir.' And he waved me right on in."

"What did you do?"

"I didn't know what to do. I tried not to make eye contact with him. I looked at the ground, said thanks, and got the hell outta there."

I sat down to wrap my mind around it. Our being "scammed" was supposed to be our get-out-of-jail-free card. It didn't occur to me that it might get us in. The supervisor must've considered how crushed we would've been to spend so much money and not see the game. When he told me, "Happens all the time," he must've been referring to the selling of fake tickets.

We sent pictures to our friends. I texted Michelle. My counterfeit ticket, assembled with tools available to anyone — thanks to her Photoshop skills — had just gotten me into the fucking Super Bowl. She couldn't believe it. Even Cecilia heard about it and texted me, "You're crazy!"

"Crazy like a fox," I replied.

We found a standing-room-only area from where we could watch the game.

But what about the woman from the picture holding the real ticket? My FedEx paper had scanned.

I had figured there was a 10-percent chance it would. I knew from my time as a ticket taker that if it did, the real ticket would no longer work. In my excitement and self-centeredness, I hadn't thought about *her*.

From that angle, I regret what I did. There's no excuse for my lack of consideration. The spin-move should never victimize a fellow fan.[28] I guess I subconsciously figured that because she had real tickets, she would be let in, regardless.

Once the stadium filled, I crept to Section 422. I peeked into the section, and found Row 14. There, in Seat 8, was the woman from the picture. I recognized the glasses and spiked hair immediately.

I didn't dare approach her; she might not have seen the humor in the story.

I loved the Super Bowl when I was a kid. At school the following day, I felt like my once-a-year-sports-fan classmates had just witnessed my world. I wanted to say, "Wasn't that fun? Don't you wanna watch more?"

But attending it was a letdown. I should've known; I had been to the NCAA Tournament and the MLB All-Star Game. National events like those are designed to be clean, perfect, and devoid of personality. Corporate types and fans of teams that aren't playing comprise a

---

28   After this realization, I revised the Spin-Move Code I described earlier, and which you can read on page 352, in the "Extra Innings" section. The only victims should be the league and the team owner — never another fan. Of course, I don't think it really does victimize sports leagues and owners. I "steal" a view and an experience of games, but do owners and leagues really own those things to begin with?

When I spin-move, yes, I reduce demand for tickets by one potential buyer. At the same time, when I buy concessions at the stadium, that's one more (overpriced) hot dog and beer that, had I not spin-moved, would've gone unsold.

significant percentage of the crowds. The neutral stadiums don't get loud. The leagues take over and sterilize videoboard productions. Those games become shows — and showcases — more than real sporting events.

In the '05 postseason, despite nice weather during games, the Astros closed their stadium's roof to keep the noise in. It became one of the loudest environments in baseball history. When they reached the World Series, Major League Baseball took over and forced them to open the roof. I'll take the conference championship game or league championship series in a raucous, partisan stadium, every time.

But there *was* a moment at the Super Bowl I'll never forget. Late in the game, Eli Manning and the Giants were trailing, with the ball deep in their own territory. Manning threw a pass down the left sideline. Cody and I saw it develop beneath us; we stood on that side of the field, at a perfect angle to see the arc of the ball, to look down and see Mario Manningham streaking toward it with defenders surrounding him, and to think: *No way he makes this catch.*

He did, and he dragged both feet in bounds. The Giants scored and won. We watched the trophy presentation, then left.

Three years later, I dug up the picture I used to make my "tickets." The accompanying newspaper article gave the woman's name and described how she had earned her tickets by winning a blood donation contest. I wanted to know how she got in. I found her phone number online.

I called one morning, and she answered on the first ring.

"You don't know me, but … "

"Conversations that begin that way are always fun," she interrupted with a chuckle.

I was pretty sure the statute of limitations for my offense had passed, but just in case, I told it as though a friend of mine had forged the tickets and recently told me the story. I was calling to verify that he wasn't making it up.

She giggled. "Good on him!" She was amazed the fakes had worked.

"Did you have any trouble getting in?" I asked.

"Nope, not at all. Tickets scanned right away. I had the time of my life." [29]

---

29   I don't know how her ticket scanned. I probably never will. But I'm grateful it did.

"Of course," Dad said. "Always have been."

Just like that, we rewrote our lifetimes of daydreaming about the World Series. It was the Blues, and the Stanley Cup, that we *really* cared about.

CHAPTER 36

THE LAST BORDER WAR:

NO. 3 MISSOURI AT NO. 4 KANSAS

LAWRENCE, KS

February 25, 2012

I gave my usual sales pitch to get Jim, Drew, and Ben to join me for the last scheduled Mizzou-kansas basketball game, before Mizzou moved to the SEC. There was no Spin-Moving 101 this time. The guys had graduated.

As we surveyed the perimeter, I noticed added layers of security at the Allen Fieldhouse media doors. One person might get through, but not four.

Around the corner, a bridge connected a parking garage to first and second-level entrances. The security alignment was the same at each: ticket takers on both sides of a 30-foot-wide entrance with no doors or turnstiles. The ticket takers weren't even in the building. They stood on the bridge, 10 feet in front of where it ended and the Fieldhouse began.

We crouched behind an SUV in the garage. I called the play.

"Drew and I are gonna take the upper deck here. Jim and Ben, you two hit downstairs. Doesn't matter how you do it, just be in the Mizzou section in 15 minutes."

Drew and I watched our friends walk down the steps.

"You wanna run left or right?" I asked.

He grinned at me, amused by how seriously I took this, and said, "I'll go right."

We crossed the bridge and I approached the ticket taker on the left. His head was down; he was scanning someone's ticket. I darted behind him, and by the time he looked up, I was gone. It was, and still is, the smoothest, purest spin-move I've executed.

I unzipped my jacket and wiggled out of the sleeves as I ran around the concourse. On the opposite side of the arena, I spotted Drew. We slipped into the nearest bathroom, and when we emerged, we were wearing Mizzou gold, with blue shirts and black jackets balled under our arms. As we approached the seating area, we saw Ben scurrying up a staircase toward us.

We found the small group of gold-clad Missouri fans in the upper deck, but Jim was missing. Again.

There were 10 minutes until tip, then five. I stood up and crossed my arms, staring at the entrance to our section. He knew where to meet us, didn't he? I should have been clearer.

As the starting lineups were announced, we saw Jim

climbing the stairs toward us, panting. When he arrived, he took a deep breath, then glared at Ben.

"You fuckin' jumped early again!"

Jim saw us looking at him eagerly. He slowed and lowered his voice to play up the drama. "In my plain, blue collared shirt, just like any kansas student reporter would wear; and with a perpetually befuddled look on my face, just as any kansas student would have, I waited outside the media door until I saw some guys with camera equipment walk out, then grabbed the door and slipped in. There was an old lady sitting at the desk, and I broke into a light jog toward the seats. I heard some stifled shouts from Granny, but no sweat."

We howled at the absurdity of it all.

We later watched a recording of the game and heard broadcaster Verne Lundquist describe the crowd. "Sixteen-thousand, two hundred, plus I'll bet a couple hundred other bodies who've squeezed in here somehow, avoided security, and are scurrying around the building."

I don't know where he got "a couple hundred," but I like thinking there were other gatecrashers at that game. And I can't help smiling at the thought of a producer telling Verne, as he prepared for the broadcast, about a security report of our spin-moves.

The Tigers blew a lead and lost in overtime. When the buzzer sounded, I sat, as I always do after an excruciating loss, unable to move, barely able to blink, for what could have been an hour.

Why, after gut-punch losses, do I wait until I'm the last one in the stands and a security guard comes to say it's time to leave? Why do I let the pain fester?

I guess for the same reason I sat and stared at the cinder block wall in my bedroom after that phone call from Cecilia, and why I thought about killing myself instead of squeezing a stress ball. For the same reason "Go Cubs Go" is a cheery tune to play after a win, but "A Dying Cub Fan's Last Request" is, by far, the more powerful song.

When we lose — when we're at our lowest, deepest, and darkest — is when we are most vulnerable, raw, and human.

I crave the pain of those moments. I want it to build up inside me, so that when the Tigers finally win, I can let it all out in a roar that shatters windows.

I even love the moment the clock hits 0:00 on another failed season. That's my chance to prove the pain can't drive me away. Soon enough, Opening Day will be here. The team will try again. And, from the same seat, with more passion than ever, so will I.

CHAPTER 37

I know exactly how old I was when my dad started slipping from interesting to insane. I can look up "Seahawks-Panthers NFC Championship" and find the date: January 22, 2006, when Connor was 11 and I was 14.

The previous night, I was up late, as usual, roaming Dad and Marie's new house, snacking from the fridge and playing computer games. I guess I woke her, and she told him to make me go to sleep earlier.

After the games, Connor and I were packing our bags to head home to Mom's. We heard a thud. We raced upstairs and saw Marie cowering in the corner of their bedroom. Our father shooed us away with flushed, red cheeks as he peeked around the side of the door and eased it closed.

I don't think I was surprised, exactly. I knew he was capable of anything if he lost his temper.

Through the door, we heard her wailing, "Never again." She had been in an abusive relationship before.

The sound of Marie's wails going from clear to muffled as our father closed the door is forever linked in my mind to the outcome of that football game; Shaun Alexander ran for over a hundred yards in the Seahawks' win.

In the car ride to Mom's house, my dad kept muttering, "It's over. It's over. It's over."

I wouldn't really understand until college, but I knew Marie — or the love of a woman in general — had been good for him. She kept him together. She kept him on the good side of the line between interesting and insane. And now it was over.

He turned around and looked at me in the back seat. With tears in his eyes and a lump in his throat, he said, "Why couldn't you just go to sleep?"

I knew that my staying up late didn't make him assault his wife. I couldn't believe he was blaming me.

But I did not respond to his question. I stared silently out the window.

CHAPTER 38

LA COPA LIBERTADORES — QUARTERFINALS:

FLUMINENSE AT BOCA JUNIORS

BUENOS AIRES, ARGENTINA

May 17, 2012

My ticket was the size of a business card, and it listed the game's date, time, and opponent, plus my seat location and proper entrance: Gate 9. The back had a magnetic strip like a credit card, but it was printed on glossy paper that whooshed when I waved it in the air.

It was my only weapon against the hordes of security. It was probably fake.

The summer after my junior year of college, I studied in Buenos Aires, where they're proud to say there are more pro soccer teams per capita than anywhere else in the world. When porteños say it's a religion, they're not exaggerating.

Boca Juniors are the biggest, most successful club in town, and they've played in the same stadium since 1940: La Bombonera — in English, "The Chocolate Box." (Supposedly, the architect once compared its shape to a box of chocolates.)

To fit La Bombonera within the boundaries of the surrounding streets, one of the stadium's sides was designed as a flat, towering wall — similar to Fenway Park's Green Monster. The way the wall deflects noise toward the field, plus the stadium's intimate size (relative to its capacity), and the intensity of Boca fans, make it one of the loudest and most intimidating places to play in the world.

Boca was playing in the Copa Libertadores tournament — the South American equivalent of the Champions League: the premier, continent-wide, club tournament. The first leg of their quarterfinal match was set for two days after my arrival in Argentina. La Bombonera, for a Copa Libertadores game, had to be the most raucous sports environment on the planet.

On my way to the stadium, I passed a man and his son on the street, peddling tickets. After negotiating, I agreed to pay 130 pesos (about $20 U.S.) for the ticket. Before handing over the money, I looked him in the eye.

"I know there are a lot of counterfeits out here. Do you promise me this is a real ticket?" I asked in Spanish.

He said, "Te prometo." I promise you.

I was skeptical $20 could buy a ticket to such an important game, but if it turned out to be fake, I would spin.

Half a mile from the stadium, fans were lining up
along a sidewalk, fenced off from the street. More than
a dozen cops stood facing the line. A perimeter of police
barricades ran in every direction. The only way to even
approach the stadium was to wait in that line. This was
the Super Bowl on steroids.

At the front of the line was a security check. Once
you got beyond that it looked like you could, finally, approach the ticket takers.

At the initial security checkpoint, a police officer performed pat-downs and ticket checks of each fan. When
I reached the front, I showed the cop my ticket and
emptied my pockets. He glanced at the ticket, frisked
me, then moved aside to let me pass. The stadium's wall
of suites loomed on my right and a row of apartment
buildings stood to my left. The street was narrow, dark,
and crowded.

As the entrances came into sight, so did more police.
Much of that force was there to stem violence and drug
dealing, both crises in Argentinean soccer. But the sheer
number of them — I couldn't even begin to estimate;
they were *everywhere* — was ridiculous. The police were
fully armed and carried riot gear: masks, polycarbon-
ate shields, batons, and who knows what else was on
their utility belts.[30] These weren't bad-stereotype, do-
nut-eating cops, either. They were serious-looking men

---

30   Maybe police officers need every item they carry, and I'm sure most of
      them are physically fit (although we've all seen plenty of overweight cops),
      but I just don't see how they can chase down someone who's in good shape
      — and whose body is pumping full of adrenaline and not weighed down
      by heavy boots and 30 pounds of handcuffs, batons, guns, pepper spray,
      radiation detectors, walkie-talkies, etc.

and women, no older than 40, with thick biceps and tree-trunk thighs. For good measure, dozens of stadium security personnel in bright yellow vests that read, "CONTROL" roamed the area.

During spin-moves in North America, I took ushers and security by surprise. But I had the feeling that Argentinean security had seen my weak-ass shit hundreds of times and would swat me away like a mosquito.

Each gate had six turnstiles, but to get there, ticket holders had to show their tickets to a cop stationed 30 feet in front of them.[31] Without a valid ticket, I couldn't even *reach* the turnstiles.

I walked up to the cop who was checking tickets in front of Gate 9. I gave him my ticket. He ripped it in half.

"Uh ... Perdón?"

"Truco." A fake.

"Why did you rip it, though?" I turned my palms upward, shrugged, and raised my eyebrows.

He said authentic tickets were made of a material that can't be torn by hand. I looked toward the sky, silently cursing the counterfeiter who had screwed me. I would call it karma for the Super Bowl, if I believed in karma.

To have any chance with this cop, I had to act cool.

"I paid a lot of money for that ticket. Obviously, I'm not from here. I just want to see glorious Boca Juniors play one game. Please ... may I go in?"

"No puedes entrar, punto." You can't enter, period.

He put my ripped truco in his pocket and pointed

---

31   Layers of security paralyze the spin-move. You can dodge one layer and then outrun it. Two layers, maybe, if they're close enough to blow by both in one burst. But three layers, evenly spaced ... there's just no way.

away from the stadium. I hung my head as I walked past the other gates and turned a corner down a street to my left. I sat on a curb and closed my eyes. If Boca didn't advance to the semifinals, the rest of my time in Argentina would be soccer offseason.

This is where I go to work. This is where legends are made.

I circled back to the street corner. I could see Gates 6, 7, 8, and 9, but at each, cops and security guards checked tickets well before the turnstiles.

Even if I managed to get beyond that first layer without a ticket, the turnstiles themselves looked impenetrable. On each was a slot into which fans inserted their tickets and waited for a green light. Once it flashed, the machine ejected the ticket, the turnstile unlocked, and the turnstile guards (a more accurate term than "ticket takers," because they didn't actually handle tickets, they just stood behind the turnstiles) moved aside to let fans enter. Their job was to make sure the machine didn't malfunction … and to stop precisely what I was about to attempt.

Gate 6 looked like the security hub. At least 15 cops swarmed in front of and behind the turnstiles. Forget about that one.

The guard who ripped my ticket would recognize me at Gate 9. Forget about that one, too.

Because Gate 8 was between two other gates, there was no way for me to squeeze behind the first layer of security from the side.

There was hope at Gate 7. To its right was Gate 8, with all of its security guards. But to its left was an opening where anyone, ticketed or not, could walk up to the stadium wall, parallel with the row of turnstiles. Separating me from them would be a hip-high metal barrier, but not a policeman. The odds were long, but not zero.

Ten minutes before kickoff, the odds improved. The man guarding the far-left turnstile went to light a cigarette on the other side of the gate. I could hop the barrier, squeeze between the far-left turnstile and the wall, haul ass up the staircase, and get lost in the crowd.

I waited for about 15 seconds, watching, analyzing, and telling myself to *go, fucking GO* — but my body wouldn't respond to my mind. Finally, with long, quick steps, I approached the metal barrier. I kept my eye on the guard and his cigarette. I was within 20 feet and my quadriceps twitched, preparing to jump over the barrier.

As I closed in, the turnstile guard ambled back to his post, dropped his cigarette, and squashed it, along with my hopes. I stopped and hunched over like I had taken a punch to the gut.

Fireworks flared to signal the home team's entrance. Possibly my lone chance to experience this crowd and environment — the zenith of the sports world — was slipping away.

The smoke from the fireworks drifted down to the street. I was desperate. The turnstile guard was back from his cigarette break, but he was now standing behind the turnstile and a little to the right, leaving a small opening between it and the wall to the left.

Maybe I could beat him to the spot. I stepped over the metal barrier, caught my balance, turned my body sideways, and shuffled laterally through the gap. Neither

surprised nor intimidated, the turnstile guard stuck his
arm out to block the gap, but I was already halfway
through. I threw my right arm up, knocking his away,
and stepped beyond the turnstile.

I turned for the staircase and leaped for the second
step. Then my momentum stopped. The guard had
flailed at me and caught the hood of my sweatshirt. My
back banged against the corner of the turnstile.

I squirmed to get away, but within seconds, I was
surrounded. One cop grabbed a shoulder, another my
left arm, a third my right hand. They pushed me against
a wall, the various hands left my body, and a single set
of hands seized my wrists and held them together behind my back.

The hands forced me to the street and pushed me
like a baby in a stroller, my feet dragging as I struggled to match their pace. We would walk right into an
Argentinean prison, I thought, as we stepped off the sidewalk and onto the street. Would I be deported? Would
my passport be revoked? How would my Spanish hold
up under the hot lights of an interrogation?

The hands and I reached the corner in silence. We
walked another block. The screams of fans inside the
stadium faded. We were alone. Suddenly, gracefully, the
hands tightened, then loosened, and pushed me to the
ground. I rolled up beside the curb. I looked over my
shoulder, expecting to see a nightstick whipping toward
my temple. Instead, the policeman was walking away.

In the space of one deep breath, terror became confusion, then relief. I blinked. I guess he had more important
things to worry about than some kid who tried to sneak

in. I pushed myself to my feet, dusted off my jeans, and marched back toward the stadium, ready for round two. But before I was within sight of the cops, I paused. It had been an impossible task. I had gotten cocky, thinking I could spin a damn fortress. I wasn't even close. Spin-moving requires complete confidence, and as much as I told myself, "C'mon, Trevor, if you're one of the greats, you'll find a way," I knew it was hopeless.

I turned down a side street and entered a pizzeria, where men strained their necks to see a 17-inch TV behind the bar. I stayed for the first half.

Before the second half started, I returned to the sidewalk outside the stadium. Inside, 50,000 people were stomping their feet and rocking the stadium to its foundations. They were locking their arms and swaying. They were chanting so loudly, the noise poured over the walls.

They were taunting me.

They were the Boca fans who had walked in without analyzing security or hopping barriers.

They were the cool kids who hung out with girls after school while I sat at home and played video games.

They were the Yankee fans who won the World Series without worrying that it would never happen.

They were my fraternity brothers who got the thing I wanted most without even trying.

They were taking part in the best sports environment on the planet, and I was sitting on the fucking curb, a virgin and a failure with a dad who died cold and alone.

With my elbows on my knees, I stared at the pavement and listened.

CHAPTER 39

Michelle was the one initiating conversation when I got back from Indianapolis. We were sharing a class that semester and had barely interacted, but now she started sitting next to me. She was *flirting* with me. She asked about the Super Bowl; about how I got away with such little effort in class; how I decided to grow a goatee; what made me tick. All with that "bemused curiosity with which a woman views a man's enthusiasms," as Frederick Exley writes in *A Fan's Notes*, that I thought was my reward for being so intense.

The Super Bowl had flipped the script, and the action was now following the one I had written in my head: Jake Taylor in *Major League* drives in the run that wins the Pennant, and Rene Russo jumps into his arms. I pull off the Super Bowl spin-move and come home a hero. Beautiful, charming girl sees how I *make shit happen*. She wants to learn more, sees that I'm brilliant, and falls for me.

I asked Michelle to a fraternity date party at a local bar. She said she was "still trying to work things out" with her boyfriend, but agreed to come. We pregamed at the house, and I casually mentioned I had brought back some wine from Israel to share. We drank it as we went from room to room.

She was wearing a stunning red dress; I was in Dad's old sport coat. A week earlier, I would have been laughed at for drinking Israeli wine and wearing a sport coat from the '80s. Sneaking into the Super Bowl was impressive, the guys had to admit, but they thought I was nuts for even trying.

But it's only crazy if it doesn't work, and it *had* worked; it won me Michelle. They couldn't laugh at me with her on my arm. I felt cool and cultured; the Spin-Move Man of Mystery. I got what I wanted because I was clever and daring and determined. I was unique. I was interesting, not insane.

Somehow, we missed the bus to the bar. We had the house to ourselves.

When she was my TA, I told her I had to miss a class for my dad's funeral. After quite a bit of wine, she asked, "How are you and your family dealing with … you know, your dad and all?"

I thought she was courageous, and sweet, for checking on me. I shrugged, as if I weren't excited to show off my inner strength. "I don't know, what else is there to do? You get over it. You move on."

We drank more. We got high. We laughed.

I spun Dad's vinyl copy of *Abbey Road* on my turntable and skipped to "Something." I lit a candle, turned off the lights, and asked her to dance. I had to reach into my pockets, without her noticing, and maneuver my erect penis under the waistband of my underwear. I wouldn't have been very mobile otherwise.

We sang along while we slow-danced and then sat on the bed with the tension building. I looked into her eyes and she looked into mine.

"What's on your mind?" she asked.

Everything was always on my mind, but she, the drop-dead gorgeous woman, was in the unique position to help me sort through it all and assuage my fear that it would ruin me.

"What does this night mean?"

"It can't mean anything." She looked away. "I'm so sorry. I shouldn't have even come."

I was drunk and hyper-animated, trying to cover my devastation.

"No, no, no, it's fine! I had to take a shot, you know?"

"Am I the Venice Girl all over again?"

I guess I told her that story.

"Just another tough loss," I said. "It's alright; some teams are cursed." I called a sober driver and rode home with her. I blacked out on a combination of alcohol, weed, and heartbreak for the rest of the night.

The next morning, in the instant between opening my eyes and gathering my wits, I had the sensation that everything had gone perfectly. But as I sat up, I began to remember the awkward ride we took back to her place; the wave goodnight; the loneliness of sitting, drunk, in the back seat and staring out the window at the stars and looking at Jesse Hall, the iconic, postcard-picture building on campus, and thinking, *Jesse's the only girl I'll ever need.* The rerun of *SportsCenter* I watched at three in the morning, because *SportsCenter* is always there for you.

That spring, the Mizzou basketball team was one of the best in the country. It was the team I had been waiting for since I was five years old. The team Dad wanted his whole life, but never got. The team that would, for the first time in school history, reach the Final Four.

But I resented the bandwagoners on campus. They hadn't been through the heartbreak that is Mizzou fandom. And I was a loyal reader of *St. Louis Game Time*, the underground program published by a few diehard Blues fans. Its slogan was: "The key to happiness is low expectations."

High hopes were noble and cute, but consistent failure teaches you that they're unrealistic and pathetic.

"Ooh, maybe this is the year!" *No, it's not. Come on. You know better than that.*

Al and I often joked about transferring our jaded outlook on sports to romance. After Michelle, I put it into practice. I still made an effort with girls, and still failed, but I dropped the bullshit pretense of "I've got a good feeling about this one ... We have a lot in common." If I was prepared for rejection, I could wrap my heart in duct tape and never get hurt.

The night before the brackets were announced, and with the Tigers coming off a Big 12 Tournament championship, a buddy and I were standing by the house drinking fountain.

"This is the fucking year," he said. "This team is so damn good."

"No height. No depth. And it's Mizzou we're talking about. We all know how this ends. Would you honestly be surprised if they lost in the first round?"

"Ha, yeah right."

"I'm serious."

"How much you wanna bet?" he asked.

"Give me odds. I'll put down $100."

"I'll take your money, sure."

"How about 60-1?" I suggested.

Vegas wound up offering no better than 45-1. My friend was overconfident and biased. Wouldn't any rational person take advantage?

"You're on," he said. We shook hands. I would probably lose the bet, but I had made my point: I was not a bandwagoner — I was a true, crusted, cynical fan because I had been through so much disappointment that I expected to lose.

The Tigers were installed as 21.5-point favorites against Norfolk St. The biggest point-spread upset in Tournament history had been 18.5 points.

Norfolk St. 86, Missouri 84 (F).

My buddy bought me a bottle of water for $3 and a bag of peanuts for $5 at the next football game. He was a poor college student back then, but now he's on the fast track to power in the sports world. Not a bad guy to have owing me $5,992.

"It's not a coincidence. We're Mizzou. We're losers and choke artists," I wrote after the game.

When it ended, I took a lap around the house. The shock and the pain on my friends' faces was comforting, in a strange way. For once, it wasn't me. If I couldn't be happy, at least I could be right.

CHAPTER 40

LA COPA LIBERTADORES — FINAL:

CORINTHIANS AT BOCA JUNIORS

BUENOS AIRES, ARGENTINA

June 27, 2012

In an abandoned warehouse near La Bombonera, a scalper handed me a season ticket holder's photo ID card. He told me to cover the man's face with my thumb when I showed it to the turnstile guard. I had to hope they wouldn't realize that while I was a young, white guy with hair and a goatee, the man on the card was old, tan, bald, and clean-shaven.

In sports, the other team is never "better." They just "wanted it more," or "outworked us." But when Boca won the match I couldn't spin, then beat a Chilean team to reach the championship round (I watched at a hostel

along the Argentina-Brazil border, on a trip to Iguazu
Falls my friends had planned), I was left with two choic-
es: Get caught again, or admit that security was better
than me. That La Bombonera was unspinnable.
    I bought a ticket for $400 USD. I would have to eat
eggs and cereal the rest of the summer, but maybe I
was maturing.
    The ID got me past the outer layers of security. I
handed it to the turnstile guard, and he put it under the
scanner. Red X. He tried again: red X. I was sure I had
been ripped off. Terrified, I jammed the card into the
ticket slot, which is designed only for thin paper tickets.
It got stuck. Apparently, season ticket holders were supposed to use the scanner atop the turnstile; other attend-
ees were supposed to put their paper tickets in the slot.
    I scratched my head and asked one of the turnstile
guards to retrieve it. He took out a keychain, unlocked
the turnstile machine, and lifted the top. Suddenly, the
cops, turnstile guards, security guards, and fans were
all looking at the idiot gringo who put an ID card in the
ticket slot.
    He grabbed the card and reattached the top of the
machine. He looked into my eyes. Then he looked down
at the card, and stared into my eyes once more.
    "Es mio." It's mine, I urged with false confidence.
"Give it back to me." He shook his head with a look that
said, *I know this isn't yours.*
    Then, inexplicably, he gave it back.
    I hustled to a different turnstile, where I held the card
under the scanner for a full three seconds. Finally: the
green checkmark. The turnstile unlocked. I ran up the

stairs as if I had spin-moved. La Bombonera was my white whale. It could slip away from me at any time.

As I ran, I noticed the chipped yellow and blue paint on the walls. I loved that each concrete step was dilapidated. It was what a stadium should be: old, intimidating, and uncomfortable. If you were a big enough fan, you would put up with it to see your team.

The stadium was packed two hours before kickoff. The night sky turned from blue to black, and for those two hours, the whole goddamn place joined in on the chants, the songs, and the foot-stomping. It was like the team would only enter the pitch if the crowd proved they wanted it badly enough. The speakers played no music. It wasn't needed.

Allen Fieldhouse in kansas ... Bryant-Denny Stadium in Alabama ... and many of the other stadiums I've spun; they rumbled with noise and passion. But that was during crucial moments, at peak intensity.

La Bombonera was *constantly* vibrating; "It beats like a heart," the saying goes. Rumbling was its baseline.

When Boca scored, I flexed my legs, trying to hold my ground so I could take it all in, as a wave of blue and yellow jumped and crashed around me, turning the concrete beneath us into a trampoline.

It was when Boca left the tunnel before the game and entered the pitch, though — with the anticipation and nerves and firework smoke and confetti swirling — that the noise level entered another stratosphere and made resoundingly clear: Being a sports fan is worth it.

CHAPTER 41

We pulled up to Mom's house the night Dad assaulted Marie, and we walked inside and pretended it was a normal Sunday evening. Dad asked to borrow the phone book.

He couldn't go back home, obviously. He couldn't stay at our house — or his parents' — because he would've had to explain. He told us he would call his best friend.

But there he was, looking up his "best friend" in the phone book. I walked into the dining room, where he sat alone, and out of Mom's earshot.

"Who are you calling?"

"I'm just gonna give George a call real quick."

"When was the last time you talked to him?"

"Oh, it's been a couple years," he said with a shrug, as if not speaking to your best friend for a couple of years were no big deal. Dad left eventually; I never found out where he went. I don't know if George answered. We never spoke about that night again.

Connor and I always called Dad quirky. Eccentric.
One of a kind. Dad referred to himself as *particular*. After
Marie left him, he became something else entirely. He
secluded himself in an outer suburb of St. Louis. Connor
and I visited every *other* weekend. We still watched the
Cardinals, Rams, and Blues, and we still ordered pizza. But his apartment, and his mind, were in disarray.
He "quit," although I suspect he lost, job after job. One
weekend he was selling paper products; the next he was
selling furniture.

Dad loved Bob Ross, who painted landscapes on TV.
We used to watch the shows together on lazy Sunday
afternoons when there were no sports on. The clack of
scalpel on palette was the most pleasing, relaxing sound
in Dad's world.

I bought a DVD online and brought it with me
one weekend.

"This is from season seven, Trev," he said. "You
should've gotten two, three, or four."

We watched it, but I could tell from his constant fid-
geting — even more than usual — that he wasn't relaxed.

One night, we were out for pizza, and after we ordered, he went to the bathroom. A minute later, I had to
go, too. I saw him slip an unopened pint of vodka into
the trashcan.

I had seen him sip beers at ballgames, but I had never
seen him *drink*. He looked up and saw that I had seen.

"Don't need it," he said. I could tell from the way he
spoke: He thought I could read his mind. He expected
me to know why he had it — because even when out for
pizza on a weekend with his sons, his mind never stopped

finding things to worry about. And he expected me to know why he didn't need it: Because he was strong and smart enough to overcome his problems with willpower. He was trying to stave off whatever was coming. He was fighting with all the strength he could muster. But once, in the middle of the night, he called me and was trying to speak. No words came through — just moans, sighs, and gibberish. I was 17, and the hardest substance I had ever tried was Coca-Cola. I didn't understand what it meant to be fucked up, but I knew his cabinet was stocked with pills. I immediately called my aunt in Phoenix. Something was wrong, but I didn't know what to do.

The one high school assignment I didn't half-ass was that sophomore English essay only my teacher saw. Mrs. Singer's prompt was, "Write about someone you feel strongly about ... You need a strong *need to say it*."

I began, "My father is not normal; I never had Ward Cleaver for a dad. He lives on his own, in his own apartment, in his own world." I continued, "My father has had a tumultuous life. Trying to follow his mind must be like playing Connect the Dots in a dryer. In the past three years, he has had seven jobs and is often unsettled and uncomfortable and squirmy — physically and mentally. He now is on about 10 different medications: cholesterol, blood pressure, sleeping pills, pain pills, caffeine pills, and so on. I probably will turn out to be a lot like him. It wouldn't surprise me in the least if I end up taking all kinds of medications."

After he died, I looked through some of his emails. One, to Pop, said: "I hope I can be as good a dad to my sons as you've been to me."

Whatever his faults, I know this for sure: He loved us as intensely as anyone has ever loved anything. He wanted to be the best dad in the world. There was nothing he wanted more. But sometimes, wanting isn't enough.

This email, also to Pop, stands out: "I am trying not to get over-stimulated or excited re: my new drug and mental health. Sometimes my mind is still fragile and it doesn't take much to turn my brain sideways. However, I am very hopeful that we have found the right combination."

Whatever the combination was, he added a heavy dose of sports. Somehow, Dad became even more dramatic about wins and losses.

I never got to tell him about the spin-move. By the time I started doing it, he wasn't healthy enough to understand why he shouldn't worry. But his phone still had some of his texts to me during Mizzou's NCAA Tournament game in Buffalo, the day Al and I hid in the garbage bin:

C'mon. Please
Give me this. I need it
Shit
Please give me a win today god almighty
I need this win today to ease my soul and
peace of mind

Mizzou won that game. They lost two days later.

CHAPTER 42

"Every time I think I'm out, they pull me back in" isn't just *Seinfeld* quoting *The Godfather*. It's also the cruelest thing about sports. If the Cardinals, down by five in the ninth, string together a one-out walk and a seeing-eye single, what do I say to Connor?

"Here we go, this is gonna be a comeback for the ages!"

In romance, all it takes is one little commonality for my brain to build delusions of grandeur.

I met Laura early in my senior year of college. I mentioned that I liked the Beatles, and she said her favorite song was the obscure "Julia." She was a diehard fan. For a second, I considered dropping to a knee right there. I asked her to coffee instead.

During our date, I told her I believed the only good rock and roll had been written between 1962 and 1979. She made a mix CD to prove me wrong. One of the songs on her CD, "Tear Down the House" (recorded in 2008 by the Avett Brothers), made me cry for the first

time since my dad's funeral, as I drove home for winter
break on an empty, rainy road.

*"Park the old car that I love the best/Inspection's due and it
won't pass the test/It's funny how I have to put it to rest/And how
one day, I will join it."*
All the elated drives in that car, celebrating Blues
overtime wins, with the stereo blasting; all the drives to
escape, as the rage boiled because life wasn't perfect; the
time I thought long and hard, on a dark, rural highway
at two in the morning about veering into the median at
a hundred miles per hour, because like father, like son;
and the drives that occupied the space between — the
ones in which I filled the tank in a middle-of-nowhere
gas station in the middle of the night and got back on
the road with aching legs and bleary eyes, because it
didn't matter *when* I reached my destination, only that
I got there. And as long as I just … kept … driving … I
would. All those moments in that car hit me at once, and
I patted the dashboard.

Was I the only one who had such wild swings in
emotion? Had my obsession with sports drilled into my
subconscious a view of life *as* sports — where everything was momentum swings and drama? Did the same
happen to Dad?

I was beginning to realize that road trips and spin-
moves were all I had to show for my time in college. The
only meager evidence that I was anything other than
ordinary. They weren't enough.

I sent back *three* mix CDs, plus a letter, critiquing her
selections. I wrote about how important music was to
me, how I remembered the first time I heard dozens

of songs, and how I should have been the DJ at Blues games because I could find the right song for any situation or mood.

I don't remember what else it said, but it was three handwritten pages of emotion and fear and honesty.

She was going to open the package on Christmas morning. I hadn't heard back by New Year's Eve. At 11:44 p.m., I texted, "Wish I could kiss you at midnight."

The text sat there like a matzo ball in a bowl of soup, without a response, for 20 days.

I sent a last-ditch message, asking her to dinner.

No reply, obviously.

When I told the story to a friend who knew her, he shook his head.

"Yeah man, I think you kinda intimidated her."

I looked at him, then closed my eyes and buried my head in my hands. I hadn't learned from my mistakes; I doubled down on them.

That night, I went into my backyard and lay face down on the frozen ground. Tears welled in my eyes, and I forced them out. It was late January, and sitting outside, alone, with Lennon's "Isolation" in my headphones was the punishment I deserved.

I fantasized about buying a bottle of cheap whiskey, returning to the backyard, and drinking it dry. The idea had a certain, twisted romance to it — the heartbroken man on his last legs looking for answers or peace or solace at the bottom of a bottle — and I no longer wondered whether I was "interesting" or "insane." This was definitive proof that the crippling loneliness I felt late at night, early in the morning, and whenever I saw my friends holding hands with their girlfriends, would be with me forever.

That I would end up like my father, because I was my father.

CHAPTER 43

The last time I saw Dad one-on-one, we met at a McDonald's down the street from his new, sad home.

He had passed out at a bank one afternoon, after taking too many pills in the wrong order or something. The doctors who had cleared the drugs out of his system recommended an "adult care center," where he could get help. I had returned from Spain and was heading back to school for my junior year.

Dad was a sharp dresser. He had more ties than he knew what to do with. He always carried a comb and handkerchief, and often checked his hair in the rearview mirror. His beard was immaculately trimmed.

But at McDonald's, he wore a scraggly beard, a plain-white t-shirt, and gym shorts. His legs were thin as tooth-picks. The only thing missing was the straightjacket.

At the register, he surveyed his coffee options.

"Trev — you see this? They get 99 cents for a small, a dollar for a medium. Who the hell's gonna get the small?"

He smiled and laughed — a spark of his old, charmingly neurotic (but not yet crazy) self.[32] We sat down and talked about Albert Pujols and the Beatles, then walked out to the parking lot.

"Well, I'll come see you the next time I'm in town," I said.

"Sounds good."

I took a deep breath. I needed to say something important, something that had been on my mind for years, but I didn't know how.

"Dad, listen. I need you to get it together."

"I'm getting better."

"Deep down, you know you're strong enough to get back to your old self ... right? You can just snap out of it if you want to, right?"

He looked at me blankly.

"I need you to do it, so I'll know I'm strong enough to do it, too."

"I'll be ok," he said, as he looked away.

It seemed like, in the past, whenever we had an important father-son moment, he made clear, direct, and loving eye contact. He wasn't going to be ok.

We hugged, and I got in my car to head back to school.

He probably had been veering toward some kind of emotional or psychological trouble all along, even during the good old days at his bachelor pad. But I was younger

---

32   They're not the scientific or politically correct terms, but I've used words like "crazy" and "insane" throughout the book because those were the ones in my mind while the story was happening. My aunt, who had her fair share of long phone conversations with Dad (and his doctors) believes he was diagnosed with clinical depression around this time. She said he also showed symptoms of various other conditions, but was never a clear-cut case.

then. I idolized him. I was willing and able to write off his problems as "eccentricities."

When Marie left him, he was forced to look out into the horizon of his life and see that it was loveless and lonely. It sealed his fate.

I was less worried about his future than I was about mine. Look where his constant intensity — his overthinking, his ups and downs, his neuroticism, and the way sports fandom poisoned his mind — had gotten him.

Everyone says it: Even if we seem different when we're young, we all become our parents.

I remembered how proud I was when he would see me adjust my glass of water by a fraction of an inch on the end-table next to the couch while we were watching a game, and say, "We're the same person, Trev."

There was no doubt in my mind: My fate was sealed, too.

CHAPTER 44

NO. 1 MICHIGAN AT NO. 3 INDIANA

BLOOMINGTON, IN

February 2, 2013

When I stepped into the veranda, 40 feet in front of
the row of ticket takers, I nearly slipped on the smooth
concrete. With each step, I had to make sure my shoes
were gripping the floor. Snow had seeped through my
sneakers, which squeaked as I approached my mark: A
man in his mid-50s.

He was shifting his weight because his feet hurt, and
he was trying to stay warm. He fidgeted with his ticket
scanner — anything to take his mind off the boredom.
He was working a part-time job that paid him to do
something he would have done for free, but to get to the
cool half of the job, when he could watch basketball, he

had to endure the monotony of taking tickets. Not so
long ago, that had been me.

It was a week after my teary breakdown over Laura.
The third-ranked Indiana Hoosiers were in the midst of
their best basketball season in years. Their fans' anger had
been simmering for nearly a decade, since Bobby Knight
was fired and the program nosedived. They finally had
something to cheer about: the biggest game in years at
Assembly Hall, where five National Championship banners, and expectations for more, hung from the rafters.
And they had a target at which they could vent that
frustration: No. 1 Michigan. If anything could compete
with the environment at kansas, this was it — especially
because the ends of the arena are indented toward the
court to deflect noise back into the barn.

At each non-student entrance, ticket takers stood in a
row, with about 10 feet between them and no turnstiles
in sight.[33] Behind them were ramps leading to safety in
the upper levels. I looked at my feet, hoping I could dry
the soles of my shoes if I glared at them long enough.

Shit works out for you, Trevor. Make it happen.

I was four strides away when the ticket taker held
out his hand for my ticket. As I drew even with him, I

---

33   Security is tighter at student entrances to college sports venues, so avoid
      them. Cops expect students to be drunk, to try to sneak alcohol in, and
      generally to be rowdier. Student sections, therefore, are where you want to
      be during the game, if possible ... but you can usually get into them from
      one of the regular sections. Some venues, though, make it difficult. In that
      case, I advise against sneaking into a student section unless you're sure.
      My worst nightmare would be to spin-move a game, then get busted while
      trying to get into the student section. Besides, it's often better to watch the
      students jump and dance in unison from a distance than to be in the middle
      of the chaos.

planted my left foot on the concrete, sucked in my gut, and threw my arms up to avoid his hand.

I tried to explode past him, but my foot slipped. He lunged and grabbed my jacket, but his grip was weaker than my momentum. I stutter-stepped to regain my balance and sprinted to an empty ramp.

The ticket taker yelled to someone, "Hey — this guy just ran in!"

The surface on the ramp was gray linoleum with raised bumps, designed to provide solid footing. I hauled ass up the first ramp, turned the corner, and flew up the second. Near the middle of the third ramp, I heard a jangling from behind. I turned around and saw a uniformed policeman running after me, his handcuffs dangling from his hip. His uniform and utility belt were bogging him down. He was reaching for the radio on his right shoulder.

I looked away from the cop and down at my feet. I only remember seeing my blue-jeaned legs pump the three most powerful strides of my life. My knees came up high, my arms churned forcefully, and my abdomen was flexed and upright, directly over my hips. Adrenaline is a hell of a drug; if I could replicate those three strides indefinitely, I could win Olympic gold.

When I regained consciousness, I was at the top of the arena and had turned two corners. I looked back and didn't see the cop.

I had studied the layout of the building.[34] One side has an upper balcony level, and that's where I wanted to

---

34   Almost every arena/stadium has a seating diagram on its website. At the very least, have a basic understanding of where each entrance leads.

be. I found the staircase, took off my jacket, and wrapped my hat inside it. I was just another college-aged kid in a red shirt.

The moment I emerged from the staircase, I locked eyes with a cop, 20 feet away. He looked like the same one. Voices raced through my head:

Run!

Be cool, man.

Look away!

Go make small talk. Ask if he knows where a bathroom is.

But the most rational voice said to give him a nod of acknowledgement and walk calmly in the other direction. Maybe he wasn't the same cop, but he surely had heard the play-by-play on his radio of the guy who "just ran in."

I was hyperventilating; even after a high-stress situation dies down, the body continues to produce adrenaline and asks for enough oxygen to support it. I took a deep breath, nodded, and walked past him. He didn't bother me.

When I felt safe, I texted friends, "I'm in."

CHAPTER 45

"Professor, can I ask you a question?"

I was sitting across the dinner table from the fraternity's faculty advisor a few days after Indiana.

"For the last couple years, I've had this ... habit? hobby? ... of sneaking into sporting events. But I'm in freaking grad school now. Is this something that's cool and funny, or dumb and immature?"

He widened his eyes and raised his eyebrows.

"How exactly do you do that?"

"Basically, I just run in."

He laughed. "Good for you if you can do it without getting caught."

"I never have — at least, nothing that would appear in a background search. But in the 'real world,' you think people will find it cool, or will they think I'm crazy?"

"If I were you, I would define a time to stop. Once you leave school, maybe. That way, later in life, you can chalk it up to youthful indiscretion."

Youthful indiscretion. It sounded good. But spin-moving was my entire boundaries-hating, diehard sports fan identity, distilled. While my friends were stacking up academic accomplishments, sexual conquests, and job offers, I could always take solace in having snuck into the Super Bowl.

I understood why people — potential employers, for example — might think spin-moves border on lunacy. But to me, they felt like the most natural thing in the world. I had the ability to sneak into awesome sporting events. I didn't hurt anyone in the process. Why not spin?

The greatest conman of all time had visited Mizzou that year. His audience, college kids who had seen the movie about his schemes, *Catch Me If You Can*, were disappointed by the real Frank Abagnale: an aging, law-abiding FBI consultant whose escapades were long over. He discussed law enforcement more than law avoidance.

He opened the floor to questions. From the middle of a crowded row, I waded into the aisle, then toward the microphone near the stage. I cleared my throat.

"From my perspective, sir, what you did best was take advantage of the holes in massive bureaucracies. Obviously, technology has improved, but what holes still exist, and hypothetically speaking, how might one acquire the skills to exploit those holes?"

The auditorium erupted in laughter, then eagerly turned its attention to Abagnale. He gave the kind of "don't be like me" non-answer you would expect from someone who parlayed sticking it to The Man into consulting for The Man.

I wasn't going to forge checks for millions of dollars or scam my way into an airplane's pilot seat. But as the end of college — and maybe the end of my spin-move career — came into focus, I developed a new goal: to become an all-time great gatecrasher.

I had cruised into The Game of the Century in college football with four friends. I beat security at the Super Bowl. The NCAA Tournament and other big-time college basketball games were a breeze. We'll get to my World Series spins. I snuck into a Wimbledon final. I was taken down at a major international soccer match, but I went down swinging. I needed two kinds of events to complete the Spin-Move Grand Slam: a golf tournament and a hockey game.

The Winter Classic hockey game on New Year's Day, 2014, was taking place at "The Big House" on the campus of the University of Michigan. The Red Wings were playing the Maple Leafs, and the NHL was expecting more than 100,000 people.

I wore seven shirts, three pairs of pants, four pairs of socks, and two winter hats to endure the 10-degree weather. But that clothing, plus the snow on the ground, made it difficult to walk. I worried I would face the same traction problem Indiana had thrown at me.

Less than two blocks from the stadium, a scalper hawked tickets on a street corner. I wanted to spin. I hadn't done it since Indiana, and a year was far too long to go between spin-moves. But out of curiosity, I asked, "How much for your cheapest single?"

"I got a single up high for a hundo."

"Ahh, too rich for my blood." I walked on.

He trotted to catch up. "Alright. How about $75?"

"That's ok, I'm set."

"Gimme $60 for it."

"No thanks." I maneuvered around him. Then he shouted, "Yours for $50." I remembered the Spin-Move Code and bought the ticket.[35]

It turned out that spinning would have been treacherous. Cops just inside the turnstiles kept close eyes on everyone who entered. Footing near the gates was slippery in my tennis shoes, whereas the cops wore snow boots.

A few months earlier, not long after Al, Jim, and my other friends graduated (while I stayed behind in grad school), we met in Athens, GA for a Mizzou-Georgia football game. Jim and I were the only ones without tickets, so before the game, we lapped the stadium. At every gate, behind the ticket takers, stood rows of police officers. They watched intently as each fan strode through the turnstiles.

"Dude, this isn't gonna work," I told Jim as we walked. He stopped, put his hand on my shoulder, and looked me in the eye.

"I haven't felt alive in six months. I wake up at the same time every day, drive to the same place, sit in the same desk, and do the same shit. Every. Day. Martha from accounting bringing in jelly doughnuts is the highlight of my week. I need this."

"I need it too. More than you know. But we will get caught. Let me show you." We circled the stadium again.

---

35   While $50 is an arbitrary amount, it serves its purpose: to keep the spin-move reserved for special games. My full Spin-Move Code can be found in the "Extra Innings" section, on page 352.

"We could obviously get past any of these ticket takers," I said at the first entrance. "But then we'd have to run horizontally — for, what's that, 35 feet? — to get around that whole row of cops, then through the gap between that pillar and the wall, which, if it's too crowded at the wrong moment ... "

"C'mon, Trev, you don't think we could time it right?"

"Too many variables. If even one of those cops plays the right angle, we'd be toast."

At the next entrance, Jim asked, "What do we think about that fence there?"

If we could climb over it without being seen, we'd have an open lane to a staircase that would lead us to freedom.

"We'd have to climb the fence in a few seconds, not snag a shoelace or shirt sleeve on the way over, jump, and stick the landing. And even if we did all that, we'd have to win a 50-50 race to the staircase."

"Damnit, you're right," Jim said.

"This time, I hate being right."

"Of all places ... who would have guessed the University of Georgia would be the one that stops us?"

We bought tickets and felt defeated — until the game started.

I try to avoid celebrating wildly in enemy territory, because I know how crushing it is when Chicago fans invade St. Louis and we Blues fans have to sit there and listen to their cheers when they score. But sometimes, I can't help it.

The Tigers scored in the fourth quarter on a lateral to wide receiver Bud Sasser, who threw it to L'Damian Washington in the end zone. We went nuts, jumping and high-fiving, as the rest of the stadium fell silent. The Tigers won, and we allowed ourselves to start dreaming about a trip to Atlanta, seven weeks later, for the SEC Championship Game.

CHAPTER 46

The day before my Game of the Century spin in Alabama during my junior year, I had run into Cecilia on campus.

"If you ever need to talk, I'm here for you," she said.

More than two months had passed since that phone call. We had only spoken once; she'd heard that my dad died and texted me condolences.

I didn't need to talk, but I wanted to see if I could win her back. She came over, and I casually mentioned that I had just spin-moved three World Series games and was leaving to do 'Bama in 18 hours. I read her the eulogy I had given at the funeral.

As she was leaving, I said, "I don't know what went on in your head between resting it on my shoulder in Venice and now. But you're not gonna find a better guy than me anytime soon."

I could see she didn't know what to say.

My buddy Drew once told me, "You can't put

everything on her. You can't expect her to solve all your problems." I knew he was right, but I couldn't stop myself from thinking of her only in terms of what she could do for me: balance out my intensity with her effervescence; be the Zelda to my F. Scott Fitzgerald, the Bond Girl to my James Bond, wrapping her arms around me, kissing my neck, and whispering sweet nothings in my ear when I felt like the world was crashing down around me; convince me that I didn't have to become my father.

I wanted to beg her. I wanted to say, "You can't do this to me." She couldn't have realized — and I felt it was too ridiculous to express — that she was my only hope of avoiding that scraggly bearded future.

But I didn't beg her. Nobody wants to hear, "I'm not insane; I'm only insane without you." I said, "You don't have to respond if you don't want." And she didn't; we parted with a hug.

For the following three semesters, I punched my left palm with my right fist. *Venice ... for a first date? What would've been wrong with that sandwich shop on campus?*

In the privacy of my journal, I had been wondering whether she still thought about me — maybe even with a tinge of regret. Jim and Al knew I hadn't gotten over her, and they told me, "On to the next one, Trev."

Jim said, "You're an almost-smart, almost- good-looking guy. With all the girls around here, you could trip and fall into someone who'd love to be with you." But suddenly, we were seniors, and all the girls I knew were about to graduate. It was starting to look like I would leave college — college! — without a girlfriend, without having sex, without so much as a blowjob. That was

pathetic, no matter how antiquated my notions of love.
I launched one toward the end zone.

"Cecilia — I always knew I would write you another
letter ... We have this attraction, this powerful chemistry between us ... It's that chemistry I've looked for
with other girls, always measuring them by the dynamic
I have with you ... If we don't seize this, our final opportunity to be together, we will have done a disservice to
ourselves and to the scores of people who can only hope
to find someone so compatible."

This time, I wanted to read it to her in person so I
could emphasize the right words by looking into her
eyes. I finished the letter as it began to rain. I texted
her, "How annoying is it when people complain when it
starts raining?!"

"I was just thinking about you!" she responded later.

I was driving to my hockey game and listening to my
"getting pumped" playlist. "Helter Skelter" shuffled onto
my stereo. I turned the volume high enough to hurt my
ears and roared a primal scream. I couldn't let her see
how badly I needed this to work, so I would get it all out,
then and there.

I texted back, "There's something I'd like to get your
thoughts on. Are you available later this week at all?"

The next night, she came over and asked, with bemused curiosity, about my Beatles records. I put one on
and said she had to lie down and close her eyes to really
hear the music.

I leaned in to kiss her, but stopped a few inches from
her lips and whispered, "You know what I would change
about this moment?"

"What?" she whispered back.

"Nothing."

I kissed her and she kissed me and it had all the emotion of Venice, plus an extra year and a half of misery. After a while, we got around to talking about why I wanted to see her. In my pregame strategy meeting with a few friends, they suggested I forget about my letter. It would be too dramatic, too intense. Fraternity Formal was coming up, and Aaron said, "Why don't you just see if she'll go with you? Don't give up all the power right off the bat."

She said she would love to go. We made out more and went for ice cream, and as she was about to go home, she gave *me* a letter. I read it later that night.

"I truly regret and feel horrible about the way I acted/treated you after our date in Venice. I think your intensity intimidated me and I ran away."

I read that part eight or nine times. I rubbed my eyes. I had never seen the crushing truth in black and white like that.

A few days earlier, I had been playing a hockey video game with a roommate, leading by two, my eyes unblinkingly focused on the TV, the controller slipping from my hands because of the sweat.

I scored to put the game away and let out a loud "Fuck yes!" then took a long, emotionally drained swig of water.

"I've got no chance," my opponent said to the other guys in the room, with a chuckle and an index finger pointing at me. "I gotta figure out how to want it that much."

I never had to worry about my intensity intimidating the Cardinals or Blues. They were sports teams. They didn't know I existed. Cecilia was a living, breathing human in front of me. Wanting her like I wanted a Blues Stanley Cup would not help. This time, I was going to learn my damn lesson.

"You are truly one of a kind," her letter continued. "I honestly have never met anyone quite like you, and I don't think I ever will."

I knew it, I knew it, I knew it: I *was* one of a kind, but in a good way — in a genuine way — not a crazy way.

"I just think our personalities are a recipe for something great, whether it be friendship or something more ... A friend of mine who happens to be a hockey fanatic passed on the wise words, 'You miss 100% of the shots you don't take.' So this is my shot, the puck is in your rink."

Jim, Al, and Aaron came home.

"Wow," Aaron said when he heard the news. "This is a new world. Trevor has a girlfriend."

With that one sentence, everything changed, just like it was supposed to. I was no longer depressed or lonely. I no longer resented other people's happiness. I had spin-moves, I had friends, I had good health ... and now I had the girl.

But I couldn't shake the feeling that *having* wasn't really what I wanted. If I had it all, why would I keep going all-in?

CHAPTER 47

One summer day in 2007 following my sophomore year of high school, I was wearing my ripped, ratty Cardinals cap with a red bird perched on a baseball bat, standing tall and proud, as if it knew the Cardinals just won the World Series. Nine months earlier, they had, in fact, won it.

I was in Chicago with a few hours to kill after a sports broadcasting conference ended, and I went to the only place I cared to see: Wrigley Field. The Cubs were off that day, so I took the stadium tour. We visited the press box, and in my mind, I could see and hear Harry Caray singing "Take Me Out to the Ballgame." We went to the left-field seats, where Ferris Bueller sat while skipping school, telling his friend, "Hey Cameron, you realize if we played by the rules, we'd be in Gym?"

The tour took us to the bleachers, where the infamous Bleacher Bums sat, day after day, and drank beer while skipping work, watching the Cubbies lose. They knew someday, "sure as god made green apples," as Caray said on the last day of a 77-83 season in 1991, "the Cubs are gonna be in the World Series." (He must've agreed with Dad; he didn't say *win* it. When your team *gets to* the World Series — or the Cup Final, or the Final Four — there are more games to look forward to. The magic carpet ride continues.)

They had been waiting to win for 99 years. If it ever happened, "Chicago will sink into Lake Michigan," I liked to say when I was young. The whole country would root for the Cubs, and the celebration would last for weeks, for months, for years. Parades. Festivals. Music. Love.

There was one view the tour hadn't covered: the one from the rooftops beyond the outfield wall, where Steve Goodman sang about hopes crushed like paper beer cups, year after year after year, in the video of "A Dying Cub Fan's Last Request" that I watched often.

Tall, locked fences guarded the staircases leading to the roofs of the apartment buildings. I dragged a recycling bin in front of one, hopped onto it, and jumped over the anti-climb spikes on top of the fence. I hustled up the stairs and took in the view.

I never told anyone what I did when I came down. It would have been too embarrassing; people knew me as the most passionate Cardinals fan they had ever met.

As I walked to the train, I passed a store selling Cubs merchandise. I saw in the windowsill a classic, dark blue hat with a red bill, and the clean, traditional Cubs logo: the red C that represented a century of dreaming about the World Series but never getting there.

It was a sudden instinct, with the beauty and emotion of that Last Request, and of Wrigley, and of the Lovable Losers in my head and heart.

I walked into that store and bought the hat.

It stayed in the bag all the way back to St. Louis. It lay in a box in my closet for 10 years. It's in storage now. It has never been worn. But for 30 seconds, I wished I weren't a fan of the Cardinals — the proud, always-successful franchise that had just won it all.

For 30 seconds, 16-year-old Trevor wished he had been born a fan of the long-suffering Chicago Cubs. The greatest moment of my life — the pinnacle of my existence, a celebration that would match my passion — would still have been ahead of me.

CHAPTER 48

"The guys were thrilled for me, and I was in shock —
still am. And also feeling a little off-guard," I wrote in
my journal, "because as long as I've known her, I've been
pursuing her. Now, I don't have to. It's a weird sensation."

After our next date, I read her my letter. We were
sitting on my bed. It was 11:11.

"Make a wish," she said as she tucked her legs under
her body and sat on them.

I closed my eyes, then opened them, and started to
say I wanted to kiss her.

"You can't say your wish out loud! That jinxes it."

"Ok, well I guess I'll just have to act on it."

"That's what I was hoping you'd say."

There was something subtle in her kiss. It was softer
than usual, more passionate. I reached under her shirt.
She gently brushed my hand away.

"What did you think was going to happen tonight?"

I smiled like I had gotten caught sneaking into better

seats at a ballgame. "I was just gonna see how far I could get." (I'll go back to my seats in the upper deck now.)

"That's not how it works."

"I know. I'm sorry — but the way you look … can you blame me?" I said. I let out a nervous exhale.

"Can I tell you something?" I asked.

"You can tell me anything."

I looked at the ceiling to gather my thoughts.

A few months earlier, I was in China with Al to cover a tennis tournament for the journalism school. I met a woman there. She and I had a drink at her hotel, and I was pretty sure if I suggested we go up to her room, it would have happened. But she and I had no long-term future, and she was older, and I was afraid.

I wanted to know if I would feel better about myself after telling my friends I "lost my V-Card." So I lied and said I did. It turned out, I felt no different.

"This is strictly between you and me. Not even Al knows."

I paused again. It wasn't too late to think of some other secret. I could have told her my favorite character in *Lion King* was Scar. That I liked the Red Wings — the Blues' biggest rivals — when I was a kid because it was fun to root for the villain. But she deserved to know.

"I'm a virgin." I covered my head with the blanket.

"Trev, you shouldn't be embarrassed. I think that's attractive. But I have to really trust someone for that."

We kissed more and when I took her home, before she got out of the car, I said, "Hey, I'm glad we had that talk."

"Me too."

I wrote later, "After so much pain, so much struggle

... I think I can finally, at last, say that I've made it. She's been great, and I feel stronger about her than I ever have. But a tiny part of me still wonders if it (the relationship, the sex) will live up to expectations. It's like now that I have it, do I still want it that badly?"

In Buenos Aires, on the off-chance we would get together, a year before we actually did, I had bought a copy of her favorite Harry Potter book in Spanish. I had this image of translating it to her as we sat together in bed.

I suggested it and she agreed, but after a paragraph, she asked, "Is this just a way to show off?"

I thought, for some reason, it would be romantic. But she was right. I *was* trying to show off. I was immature, still treating her like an object — a sounding board — to prove I was cool. Worldly. Interesting.

I wanted to take her ice-skating. I thought she would be impressed when she saw I was a good skater. We set a date, but then she remembered she was going to a concert that night.

I made dinner reservations for Valentine's Day at the nicest restaurant in town, then learned that she and her friends had scheduled a "single girls' night out" long before we exchanged our letters.

On a surprise snow day, I texted her excitedly. We would get to spend a whole day together, and snow is beautiful and romantic. She slept in and I waited for a response for five hours, shooting pool in my garage, worried I had said something wrong.

A few nights later, Aaron built a fire in our living room, which had floor-to-ceiling windows, as a light snow fell against a pitch-black sky. His girlfriend sat beside him and watched adoringly as he stoked the fire. Jim was sitting across from the fire with his girlfriend on his lap. Nearby, another roommate and his fiancé were sitting on a loveseat.

I texted Cecilia that I missed her. She was out of town. We spoke once about what would happen over the summer. She would be graduating and leaving town. I wasn't ready to leave school, and I certainly didn't want to get a job, so I had signed up to spin my wheels for a year in grad school.

She made it clear that she was against the idea of a long-distance relationship. I would have tried it. After everything we went through, I figured we could make it work. But I didn't want to seem desperate, or too intense.

I pretended not to care either way, and we "agreed" to something closer to a summer fling — with a firm deadline and a general lack of commitment — than a real relationship.

But when she was at my place, I still insisted on tidying up the bathroom before she went. I still volunteered to drive 45 minutes to her workplace, just to meet for lunch. She looked at me like I was crazy, and said, "Oh come on, you don't have to do that."

One rainy weekend afternoon that spring, I suggested we take a walk in the park. It had lots of bridges. When we got there, she asked why I suggested an outdoor activity when it was raining. I thought we loved the rain. I thought it was "our thing."

"You're supposed to get caught in it, not seek it out," she said.

CHAPTER 49

The first time Jim, Al, and I shared a class — a free speech and journalism course junior year — we screwed ourselves over.

The class wasn't interesting enough to care about, but it was difficult enough to be annoying. We were lazy, cocky, and thought we already possessed all of life's knowledge. We took turns going to class and figured we could combine our notes.

The night before the final, we met in my and Jim's room to study. I don't remember exactly how the conversation unfolded, but probably something like this:

"Gonna be honest here, guys," Jim must've said. "I went to class maybe five times all semester. Really let the team down."

Al probably opened his notebook and plopped it on the coffee table. Page one might've had a few bullet points. On page two, maybe hypothetical line combinations for the Islanders. Page three and onward? Blank.

My notes were no better.

"We knew this was gonna happen, right?" I said through laughter.

"This was the only way it could have happened," Jim said.

It was either fail or spin-move, and the choice was easy. I would sit in the back of the auditorium, get a test, and bolt for home. I would answer the questions, with a little help from some friends, and text the answers to Jim and Al. Jim would receive one test, and then, when the teacher asked, "Did anyone not get an exam?" as she always did, he would raise his hand and grab a second one. He would write my name on one, his on the other. He would fill out both and drop them at the same time into the box at the front of the auditorium.

But Jim's old phone received my messages in a jumbled order. Al, whose phone got my messages properly, finished his test and turned it in. That left Jim as the last student in the room, needing to fill out two tests while sneaking peeks at his phone, with nothing for the three teaching assistants and the professor to look at, except for him.

He couldn't do it. He stuffed the test with his name into his backpack, turned in the one that said "Trevor," and left.

"Everything that could have gone wrong, did. I don't even think I got half of the answers on yours," he told me when he got home.

"I'm more worried about you — you're gonna get a zero."

"So I'll retake this shit over the summer," he sighed.

"Well, before we give up, let me get eyes on the box of tests. If we know where it is, ya never know what might happen. Maybe I can work some magic."

I loved going into crisis-management mode — when it was other people's crises. It gave me a chance to show off how rationally I could handle them. A point guard, calmly setting up the offense for a last-second shot.

I returned to the auditorium. Luckily, the professor was still there. I followed her out to the parking lot and stood behind some bushes as she put the box in her car, on the back seat on the driver's side, and returned to her office.

Meanwhile, Jim drove with Al to an adjacent parking lot. I got in the car to be the getaway driver. Al stood watch by the door to the teachers' offices. Jim walked up to our professor's car and slid a grill scraper (borrowed from the fraternity chef) along the rubber window seal of the back door on the driver's side, prodding for a soft spot. He didn't find one.

He ran around to the front passenger door. Desperate, he applied more force — enough to slit the rubber. He slipped his test into the car. It nestled between the passenger seat and the door, nowhere near the box of tests. He ran to me in the getaway car, and we got the hell out of there.

We were counting on the professor to believe that a single test jumped out of the box, floated on a nonexistent, indoor wind at an impossible angle, and wedged between the front door and the seat.

"What if she doesn't have any passengers for the next

week? Or month? Or year?" Jim wondered. "She might find that thing a year from now."

"Imagine the look on her face when she does," I said.

A few days later, our grades were posted online. I got a 44/100 — good enough to pass the class. Jim got an A. We called Al to come to our room and when we told him the news, we burst into laughter and hugged, three guys who would do anything for each other.

I'm supposed to say, with the benefit of hindsight, I'm ashamed of what I did — that we should have gone to class, studied, and taken our tests straight up. I'm not ashamed. I'm proud.

Not that we cheated and got away with it, but because a few years after we graduated, after not having seen each other in a long time, we took a weekend trip to Myrtle Beach. Al, Connor, and I were on a 30th-floor balcony overlooking the ocean as the sun was setting. We were stoned, with beers in hand, and Jim was on his way back with barbecue. Life doesn't get any better.

Connor asked to hear the Grill Scraper Story again. When Al got to the part about how the test wedged between the seat and the door, but somehow was found, accepted, and graded, I laughed so hard my cheeks started hurting, and I couldn't breathe.

The ocean was as pure and deep a blue as you can imagine, and the sky was speckled with purple and orange and the air was fresh and cool. I was with my best friends, and for one weekend, the good old days were back. I laughed and laughed and laughed as Al told the story. Connor was cracking up, too. As I gasped for breath at the end of my laugh, for a split-second, I wanted to walk up to the railing, jump to my death, and let the waves carry my body out to sea.

I knew I would never again be so happy.

I'm proud of the Grill Scraper Story because, without hurting anyone else, we created a bond — a moment we will remember forever and describe with unreserved joy. A story that will remind us we were, once upon a time, young and stupid and carefree and invincible.

Are there other ways to create those moments? Probably. But they're more meaningful when they're against the rules — when the stakes and emotions are highest.

As graduation approached, I couldn't stop thinking that our splitting up would mean losing the chance to create new, shared memories. Would my friends be as dedicated to keeping in touch as I would be? How could we ever recapture what we had during those four years? The thought made me feel like I was going to vomit — it was gurgling up from my stomach, into my esophagus, forcing itself out, and all I could do was squeeze my wrist, close my eyes, and wait for it to pass.

My father didn't have friends. He mentioned, occasionally, boyhood playmates and college roommates, but we never met them. He never talked to them on the phone.

My friends and I went our separate ways after we graduated. Jim and I sent each other letters to stay in touch. I spoke to Al on the phone. I wanted to talk them into more cross-country trips; my goal was to never lose my fuck-it-all-let's-hit-the-road youthfulness. To avoid responsibility as long as I could.

But they got real jobs. They couldn't just hit the road. I knew that day would come, and I hated being right.

Al and I had taken one last college road trip, to New York, for the Islanders' first home playoff game in six years. "You better learn sign language if you wanna communicate in that place," one writer joked.

We tried to relive the magic — the exuberance — of the first time we made that drive. The radio played "American Pie" as we were approaching Columbia on our way home. I thought back on the defining moment of our friendship, when we instinctively, simultaneously mimed the lyrics of that song. I almost had to pull over because I couldn't see the road through my tears.

This time, Al was asleep in the passenger seat.

CHAPTER 50

Two days before we left for Fraternity Formal — a trip
to Memphis with a bunch of guys and their girlfriends
for an alcohol-soaked weekend in a nice hotel — Cecilia
texted me. "Any new info I should know?"

I worried for an hour before responding. The couple
with whom we were going to split a two-bed suite had
just backed out. Had she already heard? Did she think I
planned it that way to get her drunk and alone and take
advantage of her?

I said we'd have the room to ourselves, then added,
"Just know how much I respect you and won't jeopardize
your trust."

She was probably just wondering if we needed to leave
earlier or if I had planned things to do in Memphis.

The night before we left, I saw her best friend at a house
party. She motioned for me to join her on the porch.

"Cecilia doesn't want to be treated like a queen all
the time, you know? Lighten up ... be playful, be funny,

be spontaneous. You're a smart, good-looking guy. You need to not think so much."

I knew what she meant. Cleaning the bathroom. Dinner at fancy Italian restaurants. Insisting on picking up the check. Opening doors for her. I was still in the 1950s.

That night, I wrote in my journal, "I'm worried I can't pull that off. I know her advice is right, but I'm upset I've been playing it wrong this whole time. I'm an idiot. An overly analytical idiot."

But I did pull it off. I think.

I teased her on the drive. I sang out loud and played air guitar to the music. In Memphis, we passed a mostly empty baseball stadium, where a high-school tryout was taking place. I tried a door handle, it opened, and we went in. I smiled and said, "You're officially a spin-mover."

When she put on her dress for dinner, I exaggerated a jaw drop, then pushed my jaw back into place with my hand. After dinner, while everyone else was preparing to go out, I gritted my teeth like I had bad news and said, "Sooooo, there's this important basketball game on. Would you mind terribly if I went upstairs and watched the rest of it?"

She sighed, laughed, and said she would love to join me.

On the drive back, when the song on the radio went, *"Too young, too dumb to realize/that I should have held your hand when I had the chance,"* I reached out and took her hand without a word.

"The weekend was fantastic. Laughter and flirtiness throughout. I just want to spend as much time with her as I can before she leaves," I wrote.

Maybe I had figured it out.

A few days after Formal, I texted, "Finally recovered from last weekend haha, you going out tonight too?"

"Sure am," she said. I didn't respond because I assumed such a short answer meant she didn't want to see me.

We ran into each other at a bar.

"Hi. Don't I know you from somewhere?" I joked. "Is it … Sarah? Sandy? Samantha?"

She forced a laugh. "Hey — I think I lost my friends, I gotta go."

I stood there, plastic beer cup in my hand, staring at the brown tile floor, as she walked away. The magic carpet ride really can end, just like that.

The semester had one month left, but I think she realized — again — that "all-in" was my only gear, and decided that Formal was the finish line. I had verbally agreed it was just a fling, but I never treated it or her that way.

I spent that weekend watching TV in bed. (Granted, it was the weekend of The Masters, so I might have done that anyway.)

The following Friday, she posted a picture from a party. She was there with her ex-boyfriend. It was one in the morning, and I was at my mom's house for the weekend.

My friend Dean once suggested a movie called *High Fidelity* about the failed romances of a neurotic, obsessive man. "Save it for when you're feeling really, really shitty," he said. I watched it that night because I wanted to feel shitty.

I loved the movie, until the end. Why must every

fucking movie have a happy ending? In real life, the main character winds up pathetic and miserable. I didn't even reach for the remote to turn off the TV when the movie ended; I rolled over and fell asleep on the couch.

I wrote in my journal the next day, as it sank in that the relationship was over, "I need to realize: Even when we were together, IT SUCKED AND I WAS MISERABLE!"

I was exaggerating, obviously. I was choosing to remember the time I felt guilty for watching a Gonzaga game instead of meeting up at a bar; about the Blues game she bailed on at the last minute. I was focusing on the lack of sex and on the terrified hour I spent walking around the campus gym, sitting at weightlifting machines but not actually lifting weights, trying to decide how to word that text about the hotel room.

I knew, intellectually, that no relationship — especially not a rushed, half-assed fling — could live up to my expectations. But I *felt* it could be perfect.

The image of perfection — perfect me, perfect girl, perfect life — kept me going. It was my motivation to spin-move and to road trip and to work out. To be interesting. It was supposed to be my reward for going all-in. If that image was bullshit, what did that make me? A guy whose best stories were behind him; a dude with no ambition; a loser who wanted nothing more than to return to his dad's bachelor pad as a 12-year-old, listen to the Beatles, and watch sports all day.

"I think we should meet up and clear the air," I texted after a few days of sulking. She said she would like that.

I picked her up and we got ice cream. We sat on the roof of my car talking without much eye contact.

"I don't think we should keep going out," she said. "I just don't want anyone to get hurt." She meant me. She didn't want *me* to get hurt. "I'm sorry for not being able to confront issues. Again. I'm not very good at that."

"I'm sorry, too. For being too intense and for insisting on paying for meals and opening doors for you. I get it, in my mind, that I don't need to take things so seriously. But I always go over the top. I don't know, it's my natural setting, I guess."

"Yeah ... just in our situation, probably too much."

I dropped her off and haven't seen her since, although I did write her one more letter.

"What makes me not like anyone else is an intensity, an all-or-nothingness. It's a double-edged sword, though, because it also has intimidated more than a few people over the years ... Should I change? Should I actively work to dial down the intensity? Or do I owe it to myself *not* to change?"

"Should you change?" she wrote back. "Absolutely not!"

Over time, I gave up on the idea that somehow, we would find a way back into each other's lives. But not a day has gone by that I haven't thought about her, and Venice, and how badly I fucked up by trying to be a knight in shining armor. Sometimes I'll laugh and think, "Goddamnit, could I have been any stupider?" Sometimes, I'll stare off into the distance, replaying the whole saga in my mind. If one thing had gone differently

— one less comma in a text message, one bounce of the ball — maybe everything would have changed.

For me to make any sense of it, for me to justify the pain, I need a grand, overarching analogy to sports. So I remind myself that the Cardinals' 2006 World Series win was, ultimately, a disappointment.

I tell myself, more or less convincingly, that if Cecilia and I had ever really been together and sipped milkshakes with two straws and tenderly held hands in bed on lazy Sunday mornings, then the best moments of my life — my first time in love — would already have slipped through my fingers. Those moments, once they pass, are relegated from malleable, motivating dreams to pleasant but calcified, decaying memories.

CHAPTER 51

"It was a dump, but it was our dump," my parents and uncles liked to say about the old St. Louis Arena, where the Blues played from 1967 until 1994. "I ruined a really comfortable pair of shoes during a game against Minnesota," Dad told me more than a few times. "It was raining and the roof was leaking and there was no way to get around the puddles."

"I wish I could've seen it," I would add.

I was three years old when the Blues played their last game there. If I had a time machine and could use it only once, I think I would go back to see a playoff game at the Old Barn on a Saturday night against Chicago, with cigarette smoke clouding the air, rats crawling around the basement, beer spilled all over the concourse floor, the upper bowl swaying beneath my feet, and 17,000 companions who didn't care that they were damaging their eardrums. They just wanted a goal.

I've come to appreciate the Scottrade Center — a multipurpose facility with soft acoustics to accommodate modern fire codes and concerts. It's all I've ever known. It gets plenty loud. But ask anyone: New places just don't sound like the old ones ... with a few exceptions.

One is Seattle's football stadium — which was de-signed as an echo chamber to maximize noise. In the 2011 playoffs, it registered a "seismic event" (a minor earthquake) after Marshawn Lynch's bulldozing, 67-yard touchdown run.

Two weeks after the hockey game in Michigan that I didn't spin, the Seahawks were hosting a playoff game, and the Blues happened to be playing in nearby Vancouver. The spin-move would be my time machine.

I flew to Seattle for more money than I should've spent as a poorly paid graduate assistant, but for all I knew, the Seahawks would miss the playoffs for the next hundred years. I would be going to the game for free, and I brought sandwiches and snacks in a small draw-string bag to save a few bucks on food.

By the morning of the football game, my only pos-sessions were the wallet in my front-left jeans pocket, the phone and charger in my front-right, the hat on my head, and the clothes on my back.

It poured in Seattle that day, but I wore boots that

offered good traction in any weather. They were heavy, but I had learned my lesson from Indiana: Traction is more important than speed.

Turnstiles lined each entrance and cops lurked in the background. I hadn't spin-moved a turnstile since Nebraska, the first true spin. There were no obvious holes in the defense; they knew what they were doing.

At the end of my lap, though, I found the event center next door. Security guards stood outside checking purses, but they were not scanning tickets. Anyone, ticketed or not, could tailgate inside. A gate led into the stadium from the event center.

Six turnstiles spanned the stadium entrance, and three cops stood in front of them. But I noticed a door propped ajar, to the right of the gate. Beyond that, a busy concourse.

I strutted toward what seemed like my best chance. Ten feet away, I had a clear path. As I prepared to run, an usher popped into view, and for a blink, we made eye contact. He took his position in the doorway as I veered off. He looked like he knew what I was up to. When you're spin-moving, you feel like everyone knows it.

I made a lap around the inside of the event center, re-tied my boots, and waited behind a concrete pillar, from where I could see the door. Kickoff was still an hour away. After a minute, the usher moved aside. I moved in. My pace quickened as I drew near. When I reached the doorway, I looked to the right. The usher was there, hiding in the darkness. He stood an arm's length away. He reached out, either expecting a ticket or trying to grab me. I looked down at his arm. What caught my eye was the nametag dangling near his bulbous belly. His name was Paul. He was about 50 years old.

I turned my body sideways, facing Paul straight on, shuffled to my left, and ran. I heard Paul's voice: "Hey, wait a minute now!" I rounded the corner and found a ramp to the upper deck. I ran until I reached the top.

"I'm in," I told Connor when he answered the phone. Even with less than a third of the stadium full, he could barely hear me over the noise of the crowd.

The stadium was full by kickoff, and with the Seahawks on defense, 69,000 voices screamed together. My ears were hurting by the end of the first quarter. The winter hat in my pocket could have covered them — even the slightest protection might've helped. It stayed in my pocket because hearing so many people together, pursuing the same goal — with all-in intensity and ear-splitting noise — was why I had come.

Lynch ran for a fourth-quarter touchdown that put the game away and caused another minor earthquake. As he reached the end zone, I could feel the concrete moving beneath me. I watched the fans on the first level jump with their hands in the air and then come crashing down upon each other, a wave of humanity that was experiencing one of the greatest moments of their lives.

I got to share it with them — but not with my friends.

Afterward, I went to a bar to watch other playoff games. I ate a burger and drank a beer. I had barely slept. In the warm, humid air, I put my head down on the table and dozed off. A waitress nudged me awake.

"Can I get you a coffee, sweetie?" she asked. I was alone, exhausted, and psychologically drained — and another human being had gone out of her way for me. I remember a surge of emotion that almost brought tears at the word *sweetie.*

I said sure, drank the coffee, and went back out into the rain. Around midnight, I took a bus to the airport. The stores were all closed, so I lay down near an electrical outlet and charged my phone while I slept on the freshly polished marble floor. I woke up in the morning and flew home.

I thought I had been lonely because I didn't have a girlfriend. I was about to learn — and feel — what loneliness really was.

CHAPTER 52

Goalies are supposed to be lonely. As former Montréal Canadiens netminder Ken Dryden wrote in *The Game*: "While teams insist on togetherness … a team allows a goalie to sit by himself on planes or buses. After all, *shrug*, he's a goalie. What can you expect?"

One day a few years prior, the goalie on my fraternity's roller hockey team got sick, and I, usually a defenseman, filled in. I loved it, and I stayed in net for good. But the summer Cecilia and my friends left, I built my life around it.

I drove half an hour both ways to the only sheet of ice in the area, three times a week, and planned trips home to coincide with pickup games at local rinks. Every night, I spent an hour stretching. I eliminated bread and sweets from my diet. I read goaltending blogs and trained myself to watch only the goalies in games on TV.

I listened to "I Am a Rock" by Simon and Garfunkel. I was a rock in net, and "a rock feels no pain." I was "shielded in my armor — I touched no one and no one touched me."

Goaltending provided everything I thought a romantic relationship should: a companion I cared about deeply; a constant reminder to be the best version — physically and mentally — of myself; something to anticipate when everything else in life was going wrong. And, of course, a regular, addictive release of endorphins through an intense emotional and physical experience.

Finally, I had found another love where going all-in helped. Where I could will my way to success, like in spin-moving.

I watched Game 7 of the 2011 Stanley Cup Final while studying abroad in Spain, from 2:00 a.m. to 5:00 a.m., alone on a fellow intern's couch, because my Internet wasn't fast enough for video. The Canucks' introduction, as they walked out of the dressing room and onto the ice, gave me chills. It gave me the sounds and images that laid the foundation for my recurring fantasy during grad school.

I'm the starting goalie on the Mizzou club ice hockey team. The arena is dark, but spotlights are flashing. The sound system is blaring the intro to "Where the Streets Have No Name." The entire crowd is standing, waving their rally towels, stomping their feet, and cheering so loud that the TV cameras shake.

Cecilia is in the seats. She's not a sports fan, so she's never seen anything like this. It's the coolest goddamn thing she's ever been a part of — and I'm in the middle of it.

I lead my team onto the ice and into this madness with the measured strides of a man who is confident in himself and in control of his emotions. I do my pregame stretches. I don't ac-knowledge her presence, but I know what she doesn't, what she can't know: That she's the reason I'm there.

I kiss my posts for good luck, and she laughs — I'm crazy, in a good way. Crazy like a goalie.

The game begins and the weight of everyone's expectations is on my shoulders. My team is getting dominated, but my movements are crisp and precise. I yield nothing. I am Jonathan Quick, drop-ping into the splits as if my legs were elastic. I'm making hard saves look simple and impossible saves look effortless.

But she doesn't even register on my radar. I have moved on. I am absorbed in my new love, consumed by it, and Cecilia thinks, "Gosh, there's nothing more attractive than seeing someone im-mersed in something they love."

In the dying seconds, with a 1-0 lead, I make a sprawling, right-to-left glove save, and the crowd rises to its feet for an ovation.

I wore a rubber band on my wrist and snapped it against my skin whenever that fantasy arose. I tried to murder the thought — or at least, rip Cecilia out of it. I didn't need her anymore.

But I couldn't remove her from the thought, so she was on my mind when I sprinted the last lap on a run. She was there, fueling my 15th rep on the bench press. She was there for every save I made in pickup games in empty rinks. *Look what you missed out on. Is this good enough for you?*

CHAPTER 53

A week after Cecilia ended things the first time, in August of 2011, Jim and I — new roommates and juniors in college — skipped our afternoon classes to play golf. "There's no better place to forget your troubles than the golf course," he said.

But with each ball I sent into the woods and with each short putt I missed, I gripped my clubs tighter, swung harder, and sent balls even deeper into the woods, until, by the end of the round, I was spiking clubs into the grass. It was a microcosm of my struggles with girls: The harder you try, the more desperate and nervous you become.

In the car ride back to the fraternity, I told Jim, "I never really believed that off-the-field issues affected athletes all that much. Guess I was wrong."

I cranked the stereo's volume as high as it would go and played the Beatles: "*What goes on in your heart?/What goes on in your mind?/You are tearing me apart/When you treat me so unkind.*" I stared straight ahead, moving my eyes and hands just enough to keep the car on the road.

I was mad at myself, at Cecilia, at the world, and I was so self-focused that when my mom fainted one night that September, I wrote in my journal: "The first thought that popped into my head was how, in a sick, disgusting way, maybe it would be a good thing to have a parent die so that I can really go into a tailspin and be pitied. I've come to believe that I'm perhaps the most selfish person on the face of the planet. All I really thought about while she was fainting was myself. Terrible, I know. It's clear that I'm a pretty shitty human being."

Dad was safely tucked away in his adult care center. Text messages had become the preferred mode of communication at the right time. I could keep in touch with him without having to really engage, and without having to put up with two-hour phone calls. I didn't want to think of him with that distant, gloomy look in his eye and scraggly beard.

On the morning of October 16, 2011, Mom texted me: "Call me when you get up." She was never that short.

The previous night, I was trying to convince my friend Scott, who had graduated a year earlier, that we could pull off the first ever double-spin-move day.

"We drive through the night to Green Bay. Rams-Packers. Then we head to Milwaukee and see the Cardinals clinch the Pennant. But we gotta leave soon."

"I wanna go, but I can't risk getting arrested, man. I've had a good month at work, I can afford it — what if I just buy tickets?"

I couldn't say no. Into the night I drove while he slept in the passenger seat. He woke up somewhere in southern Wisconsin around 8:00 a.m. and offered to drive, so I could sleep. Then the text came.

"You're up early," she said when I called.

"I'm, uh, in Wisconsin for the games today."

She forced a chuckle.

"Well, I almost drove to Columbia this morning. I didn't want to have to tell you this over the phone."

I knew what was coming.

"Your dad was in a car crash yesterday afternoon."

She didn't even have to say the words.

"He's gone."

I thought about saying, "He's been barreling toward this since the night Marie left him," but I didn't.

"Um," I said, not wanting Scott to know what happened, "I can't really deal with this right now. I'll be home tomorrow, ok?"

This is the moment you've been waiting for, Trevor. Where the rubber meets the road. Your time to show if you've got what it takes to make it in this world. How are you gonna respond to true adversity?

I was in rural Wisconsin. He was dead. No tears could save him, so why bother crying?

Besides, I had been closer to him than anyone. We were "the same person." This was the one time I got to act how I wanted to act, instead of how others expected me to. I would decide for myself how, where, and when to grieve. And what would be more fitting than seeing the Rams and Cardinals back-to-back?

She could hear in my voice that my response was non-negotiable.

"Will you please at least tell your friend what happened?"

"Sure."

I didn't. It would have overshadowed the upcoming 12 hours of awesomeness for the two of us. I could handle it on my own.

It was a cool, sunny autumn morning. We parked and picked up our tickets. The tailgates; the cars parked on front lawns; all of Green Bay coming together with the Packers at home — it was the perfect place to let it sink in: My dad was dead.

Scott and I entered football's cathedral through the dark concourse. We found our section and emerged from the tunnel into the light dancing off the green façade and yellow handrails. Nothing could dampen the experience of seeing Lambeau Field for the first time.

Pop, with his dark sense of humor, enjoyed telling an old joke: "I'd like to die peacefully, in my sleep, like my uncle did ... not yelling and screaming, like the passengers in his car." At least Dad was driving alone and hit a light pole, not another car.

During the second quarter, Connor texted me.

"Mom said she told you. How you doin'?"

"A lot better than the Rams." They had just given up a 93-yard touchdown and trailed 17-0.

If I couldn't have a sense of humor about driving through three states to see my hopeless, winless team play a 5-0 powerhouse, or even about something as common and natural as death, then I really did take things too seriously.

I knew I should have been with my brother. I was the only one who could fully understand his feelings. But by carrying on with humor and toughness and practicality — by restraining the emotion until the proper time — wasn't I setting the right example? Strong-minded people can compartmentalize, and I wanted to be strong.

Scott and I went crazy for the Rams' field goal to make it 24-3. "Hey, we're right back in this thing," I sarcastically warned Packers fans around us.

After the game, we drove to Milwaukee. I had barely slept, and I was literally falling asleep at the wheel until I grabbed an energy drink.

The Cardinals won the Pennant, and we celebrated with fellow fans near the team's dugout.

I awoke the next morning, stumbled to my car, and had an eight-hour drive ahead of me. Eight hours on the open road, stereo blasting, with the cool touch of the leather steering wheel. I felt like my muscles were flexed the whole way. I thought about my brother — how was he reacting? I thought about the funeral — what would I say? I thought about whether I should act the way everyone expected me to, sad and wistful, or whether I should acknowledge that I was prepared for what had been a foregone conclusion: that Dad would burn out, that the circuitry in his brain would fry.

I stopped at school before going home.

"How many Bryan Krauses do you think there are in St. Louis?" Jim asked. He had seen in the St. Louis newspaper that a Bryan Kraus died and assumed it was a different one.

Jim and I had created a two-member club called FUF; our fucked-up fathers were a source of pride. I wanted to laugh and say, "One less than there used to be," but I could only muster, "I don't know," before looking away.

CHAPTER 54

When I finished grad school, I moved to South Carolina for a hockey broadcasting and statistical analysis internship with a minor league team.

After reading *Moneyball* as a kid, I kept up with the analytics revolution in baseball. Hockey didn't see the revolution until almost a decade later, but when it arrived, I did more than keep up; I spent most of my free time studying it. Smart bloggers (though frustratingly few NHL executives) were learning the value of ditching conventional wisdom in favor of cold, hard numbers and machine-like thinking.

It became my entire worldview.

I began to think in terms of opportunity cost: When I watched stupid Internet videos, I hated myself. Instead, I could've been working or reading a book to strengthen my mind. I thought about the marginal value of the restaurant "experience." I could eat cheaper, healthier, and faster at home.

I would leave work, run a mile to the gym, swim a mile, lift weights, then run home and stretch. My "rest days" involved sneaking onto the golf course and playing 18 holes, walking the whole way.

Every morning, I ate the same breakfast — oatmeal with fruit and protein powder. Every afternoon, I ate the same lunch — salmon, tomatoes, spinach. Every night, the same dinner: grilled chicken with broccoli, onions, peppers, eggplant, and zucchini.

I gave myself a buzz cut. I took ice-cold showers.

I read books about philosophy and science. I did not use the computer or phone within an hour of going to bed to improve my sleep quality.

I did everything alone, and I liked it that way. I didn't know many people and I didn't try to make friends. Friends want to go out to eat.

I tried, with occasional success, to avoid watching porn. I wanted to stop filling my mind with delusions of female subservience. I cursed myself when I gawked at good-looking women on the street. It was a bad habit from my days in a fraternity that objectified women. It served no purpose other than to get my hopes, and my dick, up for half a second.

I liked myself more, and felt stronger emotionally, than ever. I was Rocky Balboa, training for a fight against his inner demons, gulping down raw eggs, shunning women because "Women weaken legs," as his trainer says during a workout.

I sought to become "rational." Of course, I went over the top. During the eight months I lived in South Carolina, I did not go on a single date.

If I had truly given up on love, though, I don't think I would have spent so much time trying (and failing) to become what I thought women wanted: a well-read guy with six-pack abs who happened to be a feminist.

"I haven't been depressed about the lack of female interaction," I wrote in my journal, on New Year's Day, 2015. "I do worry that I'm a little too comfortable on my own, but not only is that not a bad thing, it's a good thing! To an outsider, though, I might be seen as a cold, perhaps lonely, pessimistic, numbers-driven, robotic person."

I did meet a woman at a yoga class. We had a nice conversation. We approached the gym exit. I had organized the words in my head: *Well, I'd love to continue our conversation sometime. Can I buy you a drink?*

In the time it took us to get to the door, I came up with a million excuses: She wasn't pretty enough; she wasn't smart enough; she didn't have the right sense of humor; she probably had a boyfriend.

We got to the exit. She leaned toward the parking lot. I said, "Nice to meet ya," and walked the other way.

It's not that I was scared of her turning me down. I was scared to reopen myself to the world. Someone out there might shatter the fragile contentment I had found by not trying or caring.

CHAPTER 55

Augusta National Golf Club is pricy, uptight, and exclusive — and has just two entrances for patrons.

As Shane Ryan wrote in *Slaying the Tiger: A Year Inside the Ropes on the New PGA Tour*:

> *I strolled around the course on Wednesday with a media member who I'm sure would prefer to remain anonymous, and he stopped me on the back nine.*
>
> *"Look down," he said. "You see any pinecones?"*
>
> *I thought it would be easy — the loblolly pines were everywhere, and so was the pine straw — but I couldn't spot even a single pinecone. What I did see were black men in white jumpsuits, one assigned to each acre, tasked with scooping up any piece of litter — which, to Augusta, apparently includes pinecones — the minute it hit the ground.*
>
> *"Now look around," my friend said again. "Find a squirrel."*
>
> *I couldn't find a squirrel. "Now look up," he said, obviously having performed this patter before. "Notice any birds?"*

At this point, I felt a low rumble of panic in my stomach. How the hell do you keep birds out?

I still hadn't spun a golf tournament, and The Masters was a big enough event to convince Jim, stuck at his desk job, to come with me.

We would spin different entrances. We would meet at the iconic 12th hole and have another one of those clenching, friendship-defining, PoliSci Hugs to remember for the rest of our lives.

Google turned up Augusta's admission "badges," outlined in purple, displaying the 12th green. Like at Super Bowls, patrons (the power brokers at Augusta insist on that term instead of "fans") wear lanyards around their necks with the badges inside. Badges are supposed to be visible at all times.[36]

I watched the opening round of the tournament on TV, focusing on the patrons in the gallery and their badges. Then I went to the library, loaded the tournament telecast on one computer and Photoshop on another, and tried to remember what the hell Michelle had done.

I printed a badge on cardstock, hole-punched the top, and hung it around my neck with yarn. It looked decent — or so I thought.

Two months earlier, I had broken my ankle playing hockey and had surgery. I had just started walking again without a boot. My plan for The Masters was to hobble to

---

36   There tend to be so many layers of security at events like The Masters, Super Bowl, and probably the Final Four and College Football Playoff games that if you're gonna try to spin one of them, you should have a fake. It doesn't have to be a good fake, but you might need something just to get past the outer layers.

the ticket takers in the walking boot I no longer needed. After likely being denied because my badge didn't have a barcode, I'd moan, "But I spent my life's savings on this!" The sympathy card had worked at the Super Bowl. Jim would do the same thing at the other entrance, but with the crutches I no longer needed. How could an usher refuse a kid with a bum leg who just pissed away a grand on a fake ticket?

With our plans set, a week before we were supposed to leave, Jim texted me.

"I'm out. Sorry dude."

"What? Why? Come on, please."

"Girlfriend is visiting. Next weekend is one of the few she can."

I waited all day for a text that said, "Just kidding." It never came. I was furious. I knew priorities would change after college, but no one loved golf more than Jim. No one (except me) loved spin-moving more.

If a girlfriend was making him choose brunch and a matinee over the biggest golf tournament in the world, maybe I should be glad I didn't have one. I prepared a response.

"I would never bail on something so important to a close friend. I'd explain how you might never have another chance to go to The Masters or how this weekend will fade into the sands of time unless you do something extraordinary with it. But nah, fuck it, you're not welcome anymore."

When Al, Jim, and Drew left school, I had told them: "You call me up, I'm dropping everything to answer that call. I love driving anyway; if you need me, I'll drive

across the damn country for you." Nothing took pre-
cedence over my friends. That level of devotion might
intimidate girls, but my friends knew me. They liked me
that way, I thought.

Years later, I read that Michel de Montaigne said
about a friend, "If absence be either more pleasant or
convenient for him, it is also more acceptable to me than
his presence." That, I realized, is how a better friend
would have acted.

But I felt jilted, and I was selfish.

I didn't send that message to Jim because I wanted his
inevitable regret to creep in organically.

And deep down, I knew friends are hard to find, and
that my father died without any.

CHAPTER 56

THE MASTERS — FINAL ROUND

AUGUSTA, GA

April 13, 2014

I arrived at Aaron's apartment in Atlanta at 9:00 a.m., napped, then watched the third round. The telecast showed patrons speed-walking from the entrances as soon as the gates opened to set up lawn chairs. Hordes of people jostled for position.

It was chaos. It was perfect.

Either the ticket takers would be so busy they wouldn't have the time or energy to turn down my sob story, or I would run in, as usual.

That night, I left Atlanta for Augusta, but as I got close, paranoia set in.

"Augusta: 30 miles."

*Jeez, Trevor: Are you really doing this? You have no idea what
security at a golf tournament is gonna look like.*

"Augusta: 20 miles."

It's called The Country Club of No for a reason.

"Augusta: 10 miles."

*You've got a laminated piece of paper on a string of yarn. You
can barely walk. Turn the fuck around.*

I checked ticket prices on my phone. At 3:35 a.m.,
a badge was available for $508. I was eight miles from
Augusta. I had enough money in my bank account,
barely, to afford the badge, plus gas to get home.

What would I write in this book? (It was just a few spin-
move stories at the time.) I crafted an excuse in my head:

"I had matured since my failed spin in Buenos Aires.
In the face of certain failure, I was no longer brash,
cocky, reckless. Instead of getting caught and risking
whatever punishment might come, I recognized an impossible task and took the smart, safe route: Buy a ticket,
enter legally, and enjoy the tournament. A wiser Trevor
had surfaced," I would've bullshitted.

I remembered Aaron's words as I walked out his door.

"Good luck, Trev. Though I know you won't need it."

I sighed. "I dunno, man."

"Dude, if there's anyone in the world who could do it,
it's you. You always find a way."

I'm sure I was projecting my own thoughts onto him,
but something in his tone made me think he was living
vicariously through me. Maybe he was bored with his
job and life, and in some way, was counting on me to
remain the guy I had been in college — to remind him
that he once was brash, cocky, and reckless, too.

Besides, I needed a golf spin on my résumé. The Masters would be my crowning achievement.

I took the exit ramp for Augusta. I stopped at a 24-hour grocery store. I bought a carton of chocolate milk and did ankle exercises in the parking lot. My ankle was stiff from the drive, but I loosened the bones enough to jump and balance on my right foot. It was as close to healthy as I could will it. A splash of adrenaline was all I needed to outrun security — if my sob story failed.

I pulled into the parking lot outside Gate 6A of prim, proper Augusta National Golf Club in my boulder of a car — with the duct tape and mismatched side-view mirrors — that had never failed me.

"What's your story?" the attendant asked.

"I've come a long way to see this tournament."

"Your car's not looking so good, huh? Might be time to get a new one."

You haven't heard the stereo.

He pointed me to a parking spot with a sightline to the front gates. I eased the seat back. It was 4:30 a.m. The gates were to open at 8:00.

I floated in and out of sleep until around 7:45, when scampering feet woke me. The gates had opened early, and patrons were streaming toward the course. There was no time to crutch to the gates or limp there in my walking boot. But I was a hockey player. I would suck up the pain and run. And I would get in.

I threw a green polo shirt over the blue one I was wearing. I slipped the "badge" around my neck and tucked it beneath my shirts. I stuffed a white hat into my left pocket. My wallet was in my right. I carried nothing else." [37]

Patrons were divided into about 15 lines, each with a metal detector, followed by a badge scanner. Ushers with walkie-talkies strolled through the lines, making announcements on bullhorns: "Take your badges out and have them in your hands. As a reminder: There is absolutely no running within Augusta National Golf Club."

Shit — there was a badge check before the metal detectors, too? And I couldn't run? I looked around. My counterfeit was too thin, too shiny, and too blurry.

Ahead of me in line, a man who stood with his family turned around. "Hey, they only allow one chair per person. You mind taking one so my eight-year-old here doesn't have to carry it through security?"

A chair might help me blend in.

"Sure thing."

The gates opened. The first layer of security consisted of two temporary security guards standing at tables in front of the metal detectors. Rent-a-cops are even less competent at securing events than police officers and permanent security guards.

As the family whose chair I carried elbowed each other to show the rent-a-cops their badges, I crept around

---

37   As of 2018, Augusta National doesn't even allow patrons to carry cell phones. Bill Pennington wrote in the *New York Times*: "There is so much you cannot do at Augusta National. No running anywhere on the grounds. No sitting on the grass near the greens. No bare feet (even when sitting down). No chairs with arms. No folding chairs. No flags. No signs. No banners. No coolers. No strollers. No radios. No standing in officially designated sitting areas. No sitting in the standing areas. No cameras. No rigid chairs. No hats worn backward. No metal golf spikes. No outsize hats. No carts. And absolutely no lying down anywhere."

them. One of the guards saw me. He looked me right in the eye, and I quickly looked away. He didn't say a word. He was either too busy, too dense, or simply didn't care enough to say anything.[38] I kept moving. I was past the first layer.

The metal detectors were next. I handed the chair to a guard, dumped my wallet and hat into the designated white box, and walked through. I gathered my belongings and looked up. About 30 feet away were the ticket takers, who sat behind desks and were reaching over them to scan badges. I looked for indications of another layer of security behind them. I saw nothing.

Chair Guy was handing his badge to the ticket taker in our lane, a middle-aged woman. She was on our right. Behind her and to the left, a path wound away from the entrance. Patrons were on that path, speed-walking toward the course.

I walked past Chair Guy, turned toward him, and thrust the chair into his hands. I was ready to run. But as he took it, he stuck out a hand to shake mine. I think he introduced himself as Paul, but it could've been Peter or Patrick. He was from Minnesota. I shook his hand and blurted, "Trevor from St. Louis." I turned toward the winding path.

---

38   Security directors often contract outside security companies to assist their staff on gamedays. Usually, employees of those companies (rent-a-cops) wear different uniforms than the people who work for the venues. To be clear, normal gameday staff is ill-prepared to stop the spin-move, but these outside employees are even less prepared. They probably don't know the venue as well as you do if you've performed basic research. Additionally, the police officers who work at sports venues are usually off-duty, even though they're dressed in full uniform. To me, they therefore seem subconsciously less engaged in their jobs and less willing to exert effort.

I thought I was free. Then, Paul-Peter-Patrick called
out, "Hey wait, you need to have your ticket scanned!"
His tone was so innocent. He actually thought it had
slipped my mind to have my badge scanned. I love when
people assume I don't know what I'm doing.

I turned around and looked at him for a second, then
at the ticket taker. I took three small, backward steps, almost into the crowd that was compressed onto the path.
Then a deeper, more authoritative voice shouted, "Get
the kid in the green shirt!"

Throughout my recovery from ankle surgery, weed
and painkillers had induced vivid, lifelike dreams. They
usually involved running, and made me feel like I was
gliding through space. My fibula churned smoothly, and
there was no pain when I pushed off the ground with my
right foot. Then I would wake up, look at my cast, and
shut my eyes, hoping I could return to the dream.

When I heard "green shirt," I ran for the first time in
nine weeks. I weaved among the patrons on the walkway. I had to step off the concrete and onto the lawn to
avoid running people over. What a shame, to tread on
such perfectly manicured grass.

Behind me, a sharp, female voice: "Hey, no running!"

I could have run forever.

"That's a great way to get kicked out," a man hissed.

"The rest of us are following the rules," someone else said.

I love the quote from the movie *Eight Men Out*, when
White Sox infielder Swede Risberg is trying to convince
Buck Weaver to throw the World Series, and Buck says,
"You just play your ballgame and I'll play mine, and

we'll see how it comes out." I would have said the same thing, if I had more time.

I slowed to a fast walk. I heard nothing but footsteps from every direction. Keys jangled ... or were they handcuffs on a policeman's waist? I could not look back. I heard more footsteps, but no more voices yelled out. No hands seized me.

I removed the green polo and put on my hat. I couldn't breathe. I reached the course and kept speed-walking away from the entrance.[39] I walked across the first fairway, then the ninth. When I reached the eighth tee, I knew I was clean.

This was my Master(s)piece: Augusta freaking National. The Country Club of No. I punched the air with my right hand and wanted to shout "Woooooo-Hoooooo" while galloping through the gallery, but the last thing you want to do is draw attention to yourself after a spin.[40]

As my heart rate slowed, I admired number eight: Yellow Jasmine. It almost brought a tear to my eye. Every detail — every blade of grass, every grain of sand — was perfect. I didn't want to take my attention away from the trees and grass, not even for a second, to massage my ankle.

I called my brother from the courtesy phones on the course and left a three-word message: "Con. I'm in."

By noon, my ankle was sore. By the time Bubba Watson

---

39   Get as far away from the scene of the spin as you can. In the fifteen minutes after a spin, stay mobile — don't trap yourself in a corner, and wherever you end up, know the fastest route into a crowd of people.

40   Follow the stadium's rules after a spin. Obviously.

won the Green Jacket that evening, it was in constant, throbbing pain. But I loved the pain. The more it hurt, the more I would appreciate my ankle when it healed.

I had my golf spin. There was no disputing it: I was an all-time great gatecrasher.[41] But Jim hadn't been there for the post-spin-move hug that would've cemented it.

During our year as roommates, we would chat as we dozed off, Jim in his lofted bed, me on my mattress on the floor. One night, he said something I shrugged off as one of those phrases that sounds good, but has no practical application. As I look back on my spin-moves, though, and remember which ones brought me the most joy — and as I've realized how hollow "being great," in and of itself, is — I understand how incisive his words were.

No matter how much I wish it weren't true, and no matter how hard I tried to change the fact, I am nothing without my friends. I need them to confirm and reaffirm my personality, and to appreciate my quirks. My dad didn't have friends, and at the end, he didn't have a wife, either. And he lost his grip on reality.

"I read this once, and it stuck with me," Jim said. "Happiness is only real when shared."

---

41   The Mount Rushmore of sports gatecrashing: James Leo "One Eye" Connelly, Hyman "Pinky" Ginsberg, Dion Rich, Scott Kerman. If you're interested in reading about them and other gatecrashers, email me with the subject line "GATECRASH" at: trevor@ticketless.pub.

CHAPTER 57

My family and I talked on the phone with the rabbi who would be presiding over Dad's funeral. She wanted to get a sense of what he was like, so she could say something appropriate at the memorial service. My mom, grandpa, aunt, and brother shared warm memories while I remained silent. After the call, the rabbi sent me what she pieced together:

As we wrestle with the way Bryan lived, the potential that wasn't met, the tragedy and mystery of his death, we wrestle with our own feelings of remorse and guilt, but remember too the peace that he must be feeling, knowing that his pain is finally over, and that in a way, some of ours is, as well.

We remember those ways in which he touched our lives and made an impact on this world. He loved music and was a beautiful pianist. The piano was like a magnet; he couldn't pass it without sitting down to play. He had a spark. He could be excited, exuberant, passionate, fun. He could be charming, funny, outgoing, confident. His boys have some of his strong points; they both have the love of sports. Connor is a talented musician. Trevor has that same passion and competitive edge.[42]

His family was always hopeful that his life would improve. They wanted so badly for him to be able to engage with the world, to be well. No one ever gave up on him. At the end of "Let It Be," Paul McCartney sings, "There will be an answer." And maybe, one day, there will be. An answer to why he had to live in the way he did, and why his life ended in the way it did. But perhaps the only thing we can do for now is to let it be.

But before our conversation had moved on to funeral logistics, I spoke up.

"Just a second here. He rooted for hurricanes to strike major cities!" I let the words linger. "Why do we have to glorify people after they're gone and gloss over the negatives? He freaking rooted for hurricanes, and he encouraged us to do it, too. He wasn't a saint, so let's not portray him that way."

"Trevor, I understand where you're coming from," the rabbi said, "and you're welcome to speak tomorrow. But you're not going to be the only one there, and it's important to allow others to grieve with good thoughts."

I was angry at Dad for inconveniencing me again, and this time, not with an embarrassing request at a restaurant I could roll my eyes at, or a phone call I could ignore. I was angry at him for telling me he would be ok. I was angry at him because we were similar in so many ways, except that talking to girls had come easily to him.

---

42   This is a ... nice way of putting it.

I was angry at him for making me too intense: for sports, for the Beatles, for everything. I was angry at him for making me love him so much. Because the more you love something, the more it hurts when it's taken away.

CHAPTER 58

STANLEY CUP PLAYOFFS — ROUND 2, GAME 4:

BRUINS AT CANADIENS

MONTRÉAL, QUEBEC

May 8, 2014

"Everywhere you go, the entire conversation in the entire city is about the game that night. There's not a pocket of the city where you can escape the fact that the Habs are playing. It's everywhere."

My friend Mike heard those words on the *Marek vs. Wyshynski* hockey podcast on a Tuesday afternoon and texted me, "Before we die, we should see a playoff game in Montréal."

I hadn't been listening to the podcast. "I know man, I was kinda thinking about going for Game 4, actually. You wanna do it?"

"How much are tickets and when is the game?"

"About $230 and 8:00 Thursday night. It's so funny we both were thinking the same thing. Great minds. You're in DC?"

"Yeah. It's a nine-hour drive, which is nothing."

"Jeez, that's a piece of cake. I'll meet you there."

"I don't know, this might be too much, too soon," he responded. "I mean I'd feel bad having you drive 16 hours by yourself. Plus the Canadiens have some good talent, they'll be in the playoffs next year."

The Canadiens cling to their French-Canadian heritage. Even though it has narrowed the pool of available candidates, they've preferred coaches who speak French, and seem willing to overpay for French-Canadian players. But guys like Guy Lafleur, Jean Béliveau, Patrick Roy, and Maurice Richard are revered on a level stars in other cities can't quite reach.

In 1955, Richard assaulted an official on the ice. When league president Clarence Campbell suspended him for the rest of the season, fans argued it was because of anti-French-Canadian racism. Despite death threats, Campbell showed up at the Montréal Forum for the team's next game. The "Richard Riot" ensued.

Violence aside, I like knowing that the identities of teams and cities can be so intertwined. It makes me feel less crazy for tying *my* identity to sports. Buenos Aires and Boca Juniors; Green Bay and the Packers; the North

Side of Chicago and the Cubs; Montréal and the Habs — they're inextricable.[43]

The Habs were playing the Bruins: the most storied rivalry in hockey. If we were going to do this, it was now or never, I told Mike.

"Alright, I'm in," he said. "Start looking for tickets."

He should've known me better than that.

We met in Buffalo the night before the game. The next day at the border, the customs agent questioned me. "You came all the way from St. Louis for a hockey game?"

"I like hockey quite a bit. Go Habs, eh?"

When we arrived at our hostel, the woman at the front desk saw my Canadiens jersey and asked if we were going to the game. Mike said yes.

"How'd you get tickets?"

"Bought one online," he said.

"I'm probably gonna spin-move," I added quietly.

She had already broken into the routine response of, "Ah, very nice," but stopped mid-sentence. "What did you say?"

"I'm planning on sneaking in."

"You're out of your mind, my friend. You'll get arrested."

Another staffer, André, had been folding bed sheets in the laundry room and overheard the conversation. He wandered over.

"You know what you should do? Go to the restaurant

---

43 I remember reading as a kid about how the Pittsburgh Steelers of the '70s and '80s epitomized the grit of the Steel City. The "Showtime" L.A. Lakers encapsulated the glamour of Hollywood. But it runs even deeper — to a theological level — in Montréal. One of the team's nicknames is "La Sainte Flanelle," the holy flannel.

connected to the arena. Security there will be much less strict," he said.

"Interesting. I'll try that, thank you."

"Everywhere else, they have security guards behind the ticket takers," he continued. I smiled. He must've had some experience with this; he understood that layers are death.

Mike picked up his ticket and we headed to the rink. An hour before puck drop, we trudged through a pep rally that was teeming with fans and chaos outside the main entrance.

"Might as well go for it now," he told me as we approached the arena doors. "Besides, I wanna see it happen."

I was anxious enough to feel the adrenaline, but calm enough to be aware of my surroundings. As we closed in on the ticket takers, though, I started feeling queasy. I couldn't see any security behind them, but I did see volunteers handing out rally towels. Would they pose a threat? I decided against the main entrance.

Mike entered with his ticket, and I retreated, back through the pep rally. I walked to the restaurant. Through the doors, I could see an entrance into the arena concourse. I walked past the bouncer, but he grabbed my shoulder.

"You got a ticket?"

"I'm meeting a friend at the bar and he has mine."

"He'll have to give it to you out here."

"Gotcha."

I walked to the third and final fan entrance. Behind each ticket taker stood a police officer. In front of each ticket taker stood a security guard with a metal-detecting wand. Layers. Bad news.

As I paced past the glass doors that opened into the veranda — where the ticket takers and security guards stood with metal detector wands — I fiddled with my phone. I was wearing jeans, a red Canadiens jersey, and a white hat.

A family of six approached, and at that moment, the cop behind one of the ticket takers walked away. I wasn't going to get a better chance.

I followed close behind the family. As the last of them entered, I pulled out my wallet, then held out my arms so the guard could scan me for metal.

I stuffed everything back into my pockets and approached the ticket taker. He was a short, bald, middle-aged man. He straddled the line between arena and not-arena, up against the right side of the doorframe. There was no turnstile.

I put my head down and took three long strides past him — then looked up, ready to run. The concourse was jam-packed. I could not run forward. To my left were the other ticket takers and security guards. I looked right; a blue concrete pillar blocked my path.

I turned around. For a split second, I looked at the ticket taker. His eyes and mouth were wide open. He was completely still.

I looked past him and through the glass doors. I could run out of the building, but then how the hell would I get back in with the whole security team on the lookout?

Instead, I walked toward him with my palms turned upward, as if I were going to turn myself in. Then I juked — faking right and Sammy-Sosa-hopping left, before running through the arm's-length space between the pillar and the ticket taker. He was too stunned to move; he neither bit on my fake nor stopped me from avoiding him for a second time.

I galloped and weaved through packs of fans as I shed my jersey and hat. I had no idea if I was chased.

On my way to meet Mike at his seat in Section 408, I spotted a ticket on the floor. I picked it up, just in case.[44] I found Mike and put my jersey back on. With no empty seats, I stood in the portal to Section 408 to watch the game. As I soon found out, they don't allow standing in Montréal.

During the first commercial break, an usher asked me to take my seat. I explained that I had broken my ankle recently and it was more comfortable for me to stand. The second commercial break, a security guard and two police officers approached. I heard one of them mutter "guy in red jersey" and "not in a seat" into his walkie-talkie.

"I need to see your ticket," one of the cops demanded.

I handed him "my" ticket.

"This is for Section 419. Why are you in 408?"

"My ankle's bothering me and I prefer standing. Figured I'd hang here, since my buddy's in this section."

"Can't have you standing. It's against fire code."

What was I gonna do if he escorted me to 419? There would be someone in that seat, probably with a bunch

---

44   Keep an eye on the floor for dropped tickets at all times. If you find one, you've got unequivocal proof you belong in the stadium. I usually don't find tickets until after games, though, when they only serve as souvenirs.

of friends. They would say, "Oh, that's our ticket, we must've dropped it." I'd be fucked.

Instead, the guard radioed a supervisor and offered me a place to stand in Section 109. The cops walked away.

"Yeah, I guess that would work," I said, hiding a smile.

I followed the guard into an elevator that said "Employees Only." He led me to a small space along a wall behind a row of wheelchairs. I thanked him, and he left me alone.

The arena didn't tremble beneath my feet — modern facilities are sturdier than old barns — but the sound system boomed and everyone in the crowd was focused. All-in. When the Canadiens lost in OT, they sighed at the same time, 21,273 together, feeling the same emotion.

I had been prepared, psychologically, for The Masters to be my last spin-move. I was almost done with grad school and the end of college was my mental stop date, so I could chalk it up to "youthful indiscretion." The pearly gates of Augusta National would have been a good one to end on.

But I wasn't able to resist Montréal, and now I didn't want to be Willie Mays with the Mets, ending his career looking foolish at the plate and slow in the outfield. I had forgotten the fundamentals of the spin-move: to look beyond the first layer and to keep moving. Like an idiot, I had stood in plain sight on an empty concourse, with no escape route. I even put the jersey back on that I had worn while running in.

It worked, but I had been clumsy. I couldn't go out like that.

CHAPTER 59

"It's not an escape, or a form of entertainment, but a different version of the world," Nick Hornby writes in *Fever Pitch*, his memoir of soccer fandom.

Like a beer-commercial-stereotype sports fan, when I see someone slip at a bar and get helped to their feet, my first instinct is to stand and clap. When I'm walking through an airport, headphones in, duffel bag slung over my shoulder, my mind's eye sees the pregame video of athletes stepping off the bus and walking into the arena, all business, in their suits and ties.

But it runs deeper for diehards. Sports allow us to choose our own version of reality. If we want to believe underdogs can win, we cite examples of incredible upsets. If we want to believe the world is out to get us, we find examples of bad refereeing against our teams. If we want to kick our feet up and watch two *other* fanbases freak out over a back-and-forth, triple-OT game for our own entertainment, instead of rooting for what will make the most people happy, or which team deserves to win — well, that's one of the foundations on which the sports industry is built.

I used sports to write off love.

My immersion in hockey statistics taught me how sports media, to sell newspapers and improve TV ratings, craft narratives: entertaining stories that don't stand up to statistical rigor. Certain teams and players being good or bad in the clutch; the idea that momentum is everything; entire seasons turning around because a coach delivered a rousing speech (never mind the other teams that received a similar one and didn't improve). And the most insidious narrative: The team that "wants it more" always wins. That games boil down to willpower and desire.

Mainstream sports media would have us believe that teams win primarily because they try harder, not because they're better or luckier. I've swallowed that shit from blowhard commentators, coaches, and athletes since before I could chew.

Jim and I made up in our monthly life-update letters, and I wrote this, a few months after The Masters:

In much the same way we create narratives around sports, we do the same with the word "love." In order to distract ourselves from inevitable loneliness, in order to take our minds off the fact that death awaits us all, we've decided to invent this concept of "love." But the feeling we describe as love is but a chemical reaction in our brains designed to encourage us to procreate. We're animals, no better than bears or giraffes or rats, and we're programmed to reproduce.

But because somewhere along the line that became a difficult reality to face, because at some point we had to differentiate ourselves from the animals, we started inventing what it means to "fall in love" or to "be in love." We see it in our movies, in our music, in our books and magazines ... and it's all just another narrative we're chained to.

I'm trying to unshackle myself from that narrative. I once believed that because I had a great first date in Venice, or because she was the first girl I cared about, it meant we had a future. I told myself those stories about what romance should be like. I was afraid to be lonely, and I clung to the narrative. But she wasn't "the girl of my dreams." It doesn't work that way. I found a girl I liked and got along well with, and then I told myself I should be dreaming about her.

As sports fans, we see this narrative bias everywhere. "Clutch player" and "grit" and "momentum" and "love" are all the same bullshit that comes from the same part of our primate brains that once credited rain dances for good harvests.

I am lonely. We all are. My life means nothing. None of ours do. Nothing happens for a reason; we're just ping-pong balls in the NBA lottery machine. And that's why I'm done looking for "love."

"I'm worried you're too comfortable on your own," Mom told me once, as I was playing video games for endless hours in the basement during high school.

"Ok, Mom." I probably didn't even look away from the TV.

"I just don't want you to be alone," she said.

I had taken solace so often — before I got to college, after I left college, and on long, lonely drives, or at busy, drunken, but no less lonely parties during college — in being comfortable on my own. In my ability to put a game on, shut out the rest of the world, and be happy about it.

I didn't realize then, and I still have not fully taken to heart, what Mom has known and probably worried about for years: My complete, conscious, even enthusiastic embrace of loneliness — my willing reversion to my high-school self — renders undeniable what we both fear.

That, in many ways, I have become Dad.

CHAPTER 60

NO. 15 NORTH CAROLINA AT NO. 4 DUKE

DURHAM, NC

February 18, 2015

"Whatcha got? ID? Fake wristband?" a Cameron Crazy asked me at his tailgate.

"I got nothin'."

"Well then your chances are nothin'."

I was no longer in school. My "youthful indiscretion" excuse was gone. But I lived in Greenville, SC, four hours from Duke's campus, and I wasn't ready to grow up. I couldn't miss my chance to see Duke-North Carolina at Cameron Indoor Stadium.

If one student section captured Young Trevor's fascination, it was Duke's Cameron Crazies. Plenty of other college basketball venues have bleachers full of students going nuts, but Cameron's rabid fans squeeze into just 9,314 seats, so it seemed more intense.

Duke has been unavoidable on ESPN since I've been a basketball fan. Dick Vitale loved to praise the Crazies. To me, they're the benchmark for rowdiness, and they would be at their loudest for a game against UNC, with both teams in the Top 15.

I set out alone on a snowy afternoon. I had read a *Wall Street Journal* article that described a secret tunnel into the arena from an auxiliary gym.[45]

I was confident, despite its insinuation that sneaking in was impossible.

I was confident, despite a knowledgeable friend's warning: "You will *not* get away with it at Cameron. It's too freakin' small. It's like a community college gym. Only so many entrances. You won't be able to just 'disappear' into the crowd. You will get arrested there, not worth it."

I was still confident when I met that student at the Duke tailgate, and he said my chances were nothin'.

"What if I told you, hypothetically, that I'm a veteran at this kind of thing?"

"Well then your chances are incredibly slim."

Good enough for me. I took a lap around the building. Behind each ticket taker was a security guard. Behind

---

45 *Want to See the Duke-UNC Game? Better Be Hiding in the Restroom Now*: "Inside the auxiliary gymnasium's side door, down the stairs to the basement, past a door that may be locked, through a dingy underground corridor, up some steps, then a steeper flight of stairs, there's a light at the end of the tunnel. It's a hidden entrance to Duke University's basketball arena. But sneaking into Cameron Indoor Stadium isn't such a slam-dunk. The few students who make it that far find a foul sight: a team in bright yellow uniforms guarding the doors."

them, on both sides of the main entrance, police officers stood watch. Even if I somehow managed to elude all of that, I couldn't see anywhere to run or hide. The only possibility seemed to be an entrance around the corner from the main one, where a staircase to the upper level sat directly behind the doors.[46]

But when the doors officially opened for the game, two security guards positioned themselves *in front of* the ticket takers at that entrance. Their sole responsibility was to make sure anyone who passed them was holding a ticket. For good measure, a police officer stood behind the ticket takers. Three layers. Impossible.

Across the street from the arena was the auxiliary gym and the "secret" entrance. The door to the tunnel that led to the arena was unlocked. I sat on the steps next to it and pretended to make a phone call while I observed. Members of Duke's band came and went. I could follow them through the tunnel, but I knew I would still have to go through at least one security checkpoint at the other end.

Three guys about my age emerged from the tunnel. They were not wearing band uniforms. As they passed me with their shoulders slumped, one of them said, "Damn, man ... "

I recognized that posture and tone of voice. "Hey, you guys tryin' to sneak in?"

---

46   An entrance with a staircase nearby is preferable to one without it, because, again: Get high as quickly as you can. If you're young and in good shape, you're faster than most stadium security, and a staircase will broaden that gap even further. Plus, put yourself in the mind of a part-time, poorly paid security guard, seeing someone bolt up the stairs. My money's on, "I ain't gonna break my damn neck chasing people around" as your response.

"Yeah, and we got into the tunnel there, but there's two guards at the top of the staircase."

"When you went up, did the guards stand in your way to stop you from running past?"

"We didn't even go up."

"Would *I* have any chance of running past?"

"Maybe, but I wouldn't try it."

They left, and I walked back across the street.

Every entrance was still on lockdown. Compared to other road trips, this four-hour drive had been nothing — a visit to the grocery store. I didn't need another spin for my "legacy;" that narrative was something I made up to convince myself I wasn't a failure — that there was at least one thing in this world I was great at. That even if I was crazy, I also had a trace of brilliance.

But I was right there — right outside the damn arena. Fuck it.

Jim once said, "Spin-moves are when you feel most alive. We gotta fight for that feeling. That's why we live." I texted him: "I should get in my car and drive home. But I'm gonna try to be a hero and I'm goin' down. At least I'll finally find out what the punishment is."

I returned to the steps beside the secret tunnel and waited. A band member opened the door to the tunnel, and before it closed, I stuck my foot between the door and doorframe. She turned around and gave a puzzled look, then shrugged and continued walking toward the arena. I followed. I had no plan; I was too jittery to think straight. I watched her climb the steps — at the top, there was only one guard, not two. He wore a bright yellow jacket; he was a rent-a-cop, not police or arena staff. A glimmer of hope.

She walked past the guard with a head nod. The guard turned his attention to me. As I climbed the staircase toward certain doom, we locked eyes. I immediately broke my gaze and looked at my shoes.

I could run past him, then keep going. It looked like that would take me onto the court.

I could run around him. There was space to the left, but I didn't know where it led.

Or, I could play it cool and walk past him. If he called out for me, I would keep walking and see what happened.

I reached the top, adrenaline prevailed, and my mind went blank. Our eyes met again. I gave a quick nod, the way two acquaintances in an office might acknowledge each other passing in a hallway. I walked past him, toward the court. I did not look back.

I emerged through a set of double doors onto the courtside bleachers. I walked up one row and down another, putting people and distance between that guard and me. I removed my sweatshirt, put on a hat, and found an empty corner of the bleachers. I looked back; no one had followed me.

As tip-off approached, the bleachers filled up. There was an extra body in my row. The man to my left was a writer for a Chicago newspaper.

"You look like a nice guy, so I'm gonna let you in on a secret. I snuck in here. I don't have a ticket. I'll make myself as small as I can, but I'm begging you, will you please tolerate a little discomfort?"

He laughed. "Your secret's safe with me."

I sent Jim a picture of the court at halftime.

"You're. A. Mad. Man." I think he meant maddeningly brilliant.

"My eardrums are hurting," I texted back. "Absurdly loud."

I sat across the court from the Cameron Crazies. Whatever they did, they did together. It was physically beautiful, to see thousands of hands waving in unison like wheat in the wind. And it was emotionally beautiful, to know that even if it was just basketball, so many people could feel joy and pain and anguish — and have fun — together.

I kept wondering if a Duke basket, rebound, or steal, or even a foul called against UNC, would result in something less than maximum volume. But every damn thing: painful, earsplitting noise.

During timeouts, I would observe the crowd, listen to the noise, and feel the rumble of the bleachers beneath my feet. Then I closed my eyes. I wanted to burn the noise and the emotion into my memory.

I hoped the game would need four, five, eight overtimes. It ended after one.

CHAPTER 61

I told the rabbi I wanted to give a eulogy. I was ready to destroy the illusions my family had about my father.

My journal entry from the night after the funeral says, "I had written a few words but realized they were far too negative."

I can't find that first draft. I've looked through all the emails I sent that month. I've searched every file on my computer. I've closed my eyes tight and tried to remember.

I probably described how he rooted for hurricanes. I probably wrote that he had no friends and died cold, alone, and miserable. I can see myself writing, "Finally, he's no longer a burden for my grandpa and aunt," and, "Finally, I'm free from him."

Then I remembered pitching in Little League practice one day. I couldn't find the strike zone, and as I grew flustered, then flat-out pissed off, I tried throwing harder. I wound up flinging baseballs over the catcher's head.

Dad, who must've gotten off work early, came to the mound in his red and black windbreaker, with his beard neatly trimmed and his hair perfectly combed. He told me, "Every pitch, look at me and take a deep breath."

He stood behind the backstop, his fingers interlaced at his belt, a slight smile on his face — the picture of cool and calm. It wasn't the most representative image of his life, but it's the one I want to keep.

"So I rewrote it altogether," my journal says. "Made it more respectful, shorter, and better."

When I was in fifth grade — we're talking 2002 — my dad, brother, and I had begun branching out from the Beatles in our musical tastes and discovered a song by a relatively obscure progressive rock band called Gypsy, who achieved some popularity in the St. Louis area in the mid-to-late '70s. We especially loved one song of theirs, called "Dead and Gone," but during the chorus, one lyric was difficult for us to discern.

Of course, as my mom can tell you, misunderstanding song lyrics was a crime you'd be wise not to commit around my dad, because he would never let you forget it. When Mom thought Lynyrd Skynyrd sang, "In Birmingham they love the grownups," instead of "governor," he laughed for 20 years.

But with this song, we three went back and forth, debating whether the word was "paid," "laid," "saved," or some other word with that hard "a" sound. We didn't reach a conclusion that day, but because my dad was so passionate and persistent about these kinds of things, he didn't stop thinking about it.

A couple days later, in the middle of my fifth-grade class, my teacher received a phone call, and my dad asked to talk to me. I abandoned whatever project I was working on and took the phone, expecting to hear him say either something very good or very bad — something that couldn't wait and warranted a phone call in the middle of the school day.

He said, "Trev, I figured it out: It's 'paid,' and I'm sure of it."

I laughed and agreed, we said goodbye, hung up, and I went back to class. I don't know how he figured it out. I don't know why he was so sure of it. But the fact that he never stopped thinking about our debate, even long after Connor and I had forgotten about it, is the essence of Bryan Kraus. The fact that he never stopped thinking about things was one of his best and most charming qualities. He wouldn't rest until an issue had been resolved. And it's certainly a trait he passed on to me.

But the fact that he never stopped thinking about things was also one of the characteristics that led to his unraveling.

Now that we can look it up on Google, I know he was right. That lyric is, "Mistakes I've made will follow me home. They won't be paid 'til I'm dead and gone."

Well, my dad made a lot of mistakes. He had a lot of issues that he could never stop thinking about. He talked to psychiatrists about them, lost sleep over them, and took medication to help overcome them. But Dad, you can finally stop thinking. All your mistakes have been paid now.

Game 1 of the World Series between the Cardinals and Rangers was the night of the funeral. Tears splashed on my keyboard as I wrote the last line.

Albert's gonna hit three for you tonight.

I gave my speech, the men pulled the cranks that controlled the pulleys holding the casket above the grave, and my father descended, an inch at a time, into the ground, first passing the piles of brown dirt on the sides of the grave, then drawing even with the green grass, before disappearing from sight. And it was that moment when it sank in: I would never see him again.

I could tough it out no longer, and I cried so hard my stomach hurt, my lungs hurt, my cheeks hurt. I buried my soaked cheeks in my brother's shoulders as I squeezed him with all my strength.

Later, I told Connor, "I don't think I've ever needed anything as much as I needed to hug you in that moment."

"It's almost like," he cracked a smile, "humans sometimes have deep feelings over non-sports stuff."

"We were alive right then. Really alive. Maybe more alive than we've ever been. You know what I mean?"

He did.

We went to someone's house and nibbled on hors d'oeuvres, but nobody was talking about what I was thinking: Would I end up like Dad?

The Cardinals won that night. The next day, Mom's coworkers must have rigged the office raffle. We "won" two tickets to Game 2 of the World Series. But Mom, Connor, and I were three people.

CHAPTER 62

WORLD SERIES GAME 2:

RANGERS AT CARDINALS

ST. LOUIS, MO

October 20, 2011

"Don't sweat it, Mom, I'll figure something out," I said before we left for the ballpark.

I hadn't told her about my burgeoning spin-move career (I had spin-moved seven times in two years since starting college), so she suspected nothing.

I always thought she felt left out because my relationship with Dad was so strong. When he would wake me up on weekends, he would stroke my hair, kneel beside my bed, and say in a soft, sing-songy voice, "Good morning, Mr. Sir. Can you say hello to your daaaaad?"

On weekdays, Mom had to be the bad guy. She would

wake me by yelling down the hallway, "Trevor! You're gonna miss the bus!"

But Dad wanted more than anything for his boys to be lifelong best friends. He considered the closeness of our relationship to be his legacy. But not just his. I hope my mom realizes that if he were alive, he would put his arm around her while watching me and Connor play basketball one-on-one, or pack up the car for yet another road trip together, and say, "Look, Karen — look what we made."

Connor knew what I had in mind.

"It's just not worth it, Trev," he whispered. "If it were Game 7, maybe. But not Game 2."

"I've never been to a World Series game, there might not be a Game 7, and we need to be together as a family. I'm doing it."

Outside the ballpark, I waved them ahead. "I'll meet you at your seats." Then I got to work.

Forty-five minutes before first pitch, I lapped the outside. One possibility was a set of glass doors near the third-base entrance. Next to the door was a staircase leading to the top of the stadium. There were no ticket takers there, but an usher guarded the area.[47]

I kept walking. At the home-plate entrance, behind the turnstiles, was a lobby with staircases and escalators leading to the main-level concourse. But maybe there were police or security at the top.

---

47   The most important reason to get to a game early is so that, even if you find an entrance that'll work, you can put it in your back pocket, look for an even better one, and return to it if you don't find something more to your liking.

At the left-field entrance, beside the row of turnstiles was an opening, guarded by a single usher, without a turnstile. The usher was stamping the hands of
smokers as they left to light up. No security presence
was behind him.

It was 30 minutes before first pitch. The concourse
was busy enough for me to blend in with the crowd,
but not congested enough to prevent me from reaching full speed.

I walked toward the usher, a man with white hair,
probably in his 50s. I reached into my pocket and pulled
out a ticket from a game I had attended two years prior.
He looked down to unfold the ticket. I pushed off hard
with my left foot and sprinted.

The usher yelled, "Young man!" I didn't look back. I
weaved around fellow Cardinals fans, turned the corner
to my left, slowed to a jog, and went into a bathroom to
change clothes. I removed my hat and black jacket; underneath, I wore a red and white Cardinals windbreaker.

"How much did you pay?" Mom asked when I got
to the seats.

"Well, they were going for about $300," I said truth-
fully. "So I slipped the ticket taker $20 to let me in," I lied.

She looked at me with furrowed eyebrows but said
nothing. I didn't know if she believed me, but she didn't
seem to disbelieve, either. I made a comment about the
lineup, and when she turned away, winked at Connor.

The cliché says that sports provide an escape from
real life, but when they dominate your worldview, like
they do mine, there's nothing to escape into. I would
have been locked into that game even if Dad's funeral

hadn't been 31 hours earlier. It felt like just another night at the ballpark. What I remember most clearly is Cecilia texting me that she heard what happened and was sorry for my loss.

La Russa chose not to walk All-Star Michael Young in the ninth. I was irate. "Con, what the hell is going on … why is he not putting him on first base?"

Young drove in the winning run, and the Cardinals lost. As we left the stadium, I asked fans around me, "Can you believe they didn't walk Young?" All I got were shrugs. Even the radio hosts on the post-game show weren't as emotional as I was when I called in to rant.

I knew only one person who would have matched my intensity. I wanted to call him instead.

CHAPTER 63   297

CHAPTER 63

WORLD SERIES GAME 4:

CARDINALS AT RANGERS

ARLINGTON, TX

October 23, 2011

"Is your dad coming in?" I was asked repeatedly the next day.

Dads' Weekend at the fraternity was coming up. I hadn't told many people what happened to mine.

"Nah, I don't think he can make it," I chuckled.

On Saturday morning, at our tailgate before the Mizzou football game, the 60 or so dads who did make it were dressed in sharp collared shirts and khaki pants. They sipped beers responsibly. They were lawyers, accountants, and financial advisors. Their sons were in school, their wives were loving, their yards were

well manicured, and their portfolios were diversified.
I could see the resemblance in their sons, and in their
sons' futures.

I went to the game with a friend from out of town
and was telling him about going to both the Rams and
Cardinals games in Wisconsin the previous weekend.

"You know, the Cardinals are in this little thing
called the World Series, and they play tomorrow night in
Dallas. Guess who the Rams play tomorrow afternoon."

Charlie thought for a second. "Cowboys."

"Yup. I've been thinking about it all week. Wanna go?"

Charlie laughed. "You gonna do your spin-move?"

"We should get tickets for the Rams ... it's just a regular season game. But the World Series? Yeah, why not?"

"I gotta be back at school by Monday. Think we
could make it?"

"Oh, easily. Leave Dallas after the baseball game
ends, drive through the night, no problem."

"Let me call my mom."

I nudged him as he dialed. "If it sounds like she's not
gonna go for it, tell her it's Dads' Weekend at my fraternity and you think it'd be good for me to get away."

Dad would have wanted me to get *something* out
of his death.

Charlie's mom said he could go, and when the
Mizzou game ended, we bought tickets online to the
Rams game and hit the road. We listened to Game 3
of the World Series on the radio. Albert actually did hit
three home runs.

We got to Dallas the next morning, and Charlie bought
a $400 ticket to the baseball game from a "licensed

redistributor" that operated out of a gas station. "I have a scholarship to lose," he said. "I just can't do the spin."

"I think you're gonna regret it when you see how easy it is."

"You're right — but I would get there and probably chicken out."

The Rams got clobbered, and we hurried across the parking lot to the ballpark. Between main entrances was a small gate, above which a sign read "Exit Only." An elderly woman in an usher's vest stood there. I crept to the side of the gate as I faked a phone call. Charlie watched over his shoulder as he walked toward the turnstiles.

"Meet me by third base," I said into the phone. I covered my non-phone ear with my non-phone hand. "Okay, see you there," I said to no one. I approached the usher.

"Excuse me," I said pleasantly, as I returned my phone to my pocket. The usher looked at me with a ready-to-help smile. "Where is the … "

I darted through the gate. I turned left, skipped around fans in the concourse, and did not look back. I took off my blue Rams jersey. Underneath, I was wearing Cardinal Red.

I wanted to get to the upper deck, but I had seen no staircases — only crowded escalators. I walked into a lower-level section on the other side of the ballpark from where I had spin-moved. I sat down and kicked back. It was a warm, fall night, and the sun was setting over the Ballpark in Arlington — one of the few truly pretty, retro-style new ballparks, as Dad said.

I got up after five minutes, confident I had escaped

pursuit — if there was any.[48] I took the escalator and plopped into Charlie's ticketed seat. Seconds later, I saw him climbing the stairs toward me. He hurried into our row and sat in the empty seat next to me.

"The usher — she was shocked! At first, she took a half-step after you, but then she threw her hands up ... and watched you fade into the distance."

I didn't know what to say, so I shrugged.

"That was the most badass thing I've ever seen," he whispered.

---

48   I didn't know it at the time, but former president George W. Bush threw out the first pitch. Former presidents get lifetime Secret Service protection, so some very serious people might still have been looking for me. Oh well.

CHAPTER 64

WORLD SERIES GAME 7:

RANGERS AT CARDINALS

ST. LOUIS, MO

October 28, 2011

Game 7 was in St. Louis. I met my brother at home
that afternoon.

"So … any plans for tonight?" I deadpanned.

"Yeah, there's a few cooking shows I wanna watch."

"But seriously: Let's go down there. We can just soak
up the atmosphere."

"No, no, Trev. I know you. I'm not spin-moving."

"Dude, it's gonna be so easy!"

"I would love to. I just … don't think I'd actually be
able to do it."

"Look. Let's go down there and take a walk around

the ballpark. If you don't think it's doable, we won't. I'll stay with you and not go in. I won't leave you hanging."

"Fair enough."

With Mom still at work, we went downtown. I drove toward our usual, free parking lot; five orange cones were blocking it.

"Oh yeah, that's gonna stop us." I rolled my eyes. Connor got out, tossed the cones aside, and we parked.

Before Game 2, I had noticed the glass doors by the third-base entrance. The staircase beside them was tantalizing. We went to those doors and stood there, Connor behind me, waiting for me to say or do something.

Watching over my brother — my baby brother — keeping him safe, and helping him learn from my mistakes has always been my most important job. I hope it always will be.

I had to go first. He had to feed off my confidence.

"Stay right behind me and follow my lead," I told him. "You cannot hesitate or look back."

I caught the eye of the usher inside, a man in a wheelchair, maybe in his early 40s. When he looked away, I tried opening the door. It was locked. We waited to the side. I thought we were out of the usher's sight, but he and I made eye contact again. Was there any chance he knew what I was waiting for?

I saw four men in business suits inside the stadium — front office employees, most likely — coming our way. They were going to exit through our doors. Connor and I exchanged a brief, mischievous look that said: "It's game time."

The first guy opened the door, and once the fourth

man passed through, the usher, who had been holding it open, took his hand away, allowing the door to close. Before it did, I reached out, threw it open, and ran in.

My eyes were on the staircase inside. I sprang up the first flight three steps at a time, and only upon reaching the second flight did I hear the usher's "Hey!"

I peeked over my shoulder. Connor was close behind. We arrived on the upper-level concourse and ducked into the nearest restroom. We removed our black jackets and balled them under our arms.

My brother — my pure, innocent little brother — had been unflappable on his first spin-move. I was ecstatic. It was my first true spin-move with someone else.

We found a standing-room-only area along the first-base line. All that remained was for the Cardinals to win.

When Allen Craig caught the fly ball to left, the stadium erupted — not as loudly as the Old Ballpark probably would have, but for once, I wasn't upset that it wasn't perfect. Hands rose, cheers erupted, and fans danced in the aisles.

I stood silent and contemplative amidst the madness. My eyes watered. I looked at Connor. His had, too. We hugged again.

Between firework blasts, Connor spoke.

"Dad would have loved this."

This. The Cardinals winning the World Series; our spin-move; and that we loved each other enough to do it together.

Built-in, lifelong best friends, Dad always called us.

He was right.

CHAPTER 65

When I look at the picture of me and Connor celebrating after Game 7, the first thing I see is the white headphone cord dangling from my shirt. The Blues played a regular season game that night in Calgary. I listened on the radio. You're gonna think I'm nuts, but it's true: *That* game was more important. To me, anyway.

I had already seen the Cardinals win the World Series. The second title of my lifetime was powerful because our dad had just died, and because we spin-moved the clinching game. But I hadn't been dreaming of the final out for a decade. I hadn't watched every game that year. I wasn't desperate for the Cardinals to win.

The Blues have never won the Stanley Cup. I love that about them. I like having their first title — that moment of euphoria and joy and relief — in the future, instead of in the past. If it happens, I'll know I was with them, all-in, all the way, even for dreary, early-season, 3-1 losses in Calgary. That's what will make it meaningful.

Sports have infected my mind. Like father, like son. But when I was at my lowest — borderline suicidal — what helped me most was knowing that I still had my first love, first girlfriend, and first sexual experience ahead of me.

"I'm so freaking jealous of you two," Dad said often when he introduced us to a new song or album. "Do you realize you're about to hear *Sergeant Pepper* for the first time? You know what I'd give to do that?"

We didn't.

"Oh, and you get to see your ballclub win the World Series for the first time? It's just not fair, you guys!"

In 2017, with my philosophy about the downsides of winning and the upsides of losing more fully formed, Gonzaga put it to the test. The night they advanced to the Final Four was one of the best of my life. I celebrated with Connor and a friend, a fellow diehard Zags fan who had driven to St. Louis from Chicago to watch with us. When the final buzzer sounded, we popped champagne and hugged and played "I Feel Fine" as loud as the stereo could. We went to a bar in our Gonzaga gear. We drank heavily and high-fived strangers. I danced on a dance floor — without being dragged — for probably the first time ever. We ate greasy food at a late-night diner, and we rewatched the game at home while eating cheesecake.

I wasn't thinking about the next morning, but it was marching toward us, and it arrived much too fast, with all its real-life responsibilities. We had to track down our buddy's wallet. I smashed my finger in a car door. No

elation could dull that pain. Winning was not the cure-
all I hoped it would be.

The day of the National Championship Game, I
stewed in my apartment, wondering whether I cared
more about winning or my fandom — my identity as
diehardest of the diehards. Whether I cared more about
the journey or the destination. I knew if the Zags won,
my fandom would drop from 100% intensity to 95%, because there's no time like the first time. And I knew those
last few percentage points are what make me who I am.

Before the game, I sat across from my brother
at Talayna's, the restaurant Dad took us to every
Championship Monday.

"I just don't know, Con. Call it a coping mechanism
or whatever, but we already got to the Final Four mountaintop. I want to have a new mountaintop to shoot for
next year. Something to chase. Something that will keep
us going all-in. Alexander the Great wept when there
were no more worlds to conquer. Spock said, 'Having is
not so pleasing a thing as wanting.'"

Connor thought for a second. "We might never be
back here again. It's really fucking hard to get here.
What if we lose tonight, then go our whole lives and they
never make it back?"

"You're right. But we can find meaning in that, too.
The futile struggle. There's strength and beauty there.
Sisyphus rolling the boulder up the hill. 'One must
imagine him happy.'"

"Trev, you're honestly telling me you'd be sad if they
win tonight? Come on, not even you are that psychotic."

"Can't I be both happy because something I've

wanted my whole life has happened ... and sad because it's the passing of something delicate, something that's precious to me?"

"Imagine if they win. We're gonna have that memory for the rest of our lives. It doesn't have to pass."

"Yeah, but moving forward, a dream is more useful than a memory. Do you realize Gonzaga basketball is the best thing I have going for me right now? When I'm at the gym, I play the NCAA on CBS theme song on my phone. I see the TV in my mind. Pangos is warming up for a Tournament game, and it's got that little countdown to tip-off in the bottom corner, and then it cuts to the guys in the studio previewing the game, and in that moment, I can plank longer, run faster, and do more push-ups, because I'm just so fucking pumped. I'm invincible. I don't want to lose that feeling."

When the game started, I found myself rooting like hell for the Zags — perhaps not as loudly as usual, but no existential crisis could have made me root against them.

Late in the game, they had a lead. The dream was within reach, and I wanted it with all my heart. As the lead disappeared, and then as North Carolina pulled away, I wore my devastated, motionless, sulking stare. But when it ended, I put my arm around my baby brother.

"Embrace this feeling, Con. The more it hurts now, the better it'll feel when they finally do it. Our first championship is still to come."

He was too sad to speak, but I imagined him saying, "You sound like Dad."

CHAPTER 66

THE FINAL OPENING DAY:

SEAHAWKS AT RAMS

ST. LOUIS, MO

September 13, 2015

I have no plans to officially retire from spin-moving.

I would consider spinning the Olympics. I was in Russia during the 2018 soccer World Cup. I scouted security. I would have gotten arrested had I tried to spin-move, but I didn't really *care* to try. It would have been solely to add a line to my résumé.

If I could set up a road trip to a Michigan-Ohio St. football game with both teams in the top five, or another Game of the Century between LSU and Alabama — but this time, one of those famously raucous night games at

Death Valley in Baton Rouge — I would think about spin-moving those, too. But I would want my friends to be there, either on the road trip or during the spin-move itself. Sports and spin-moves are, ultimately, just excuses to make memories with the people you love. It was our group hug outside of Section GG after the five of us spin-moved the Alabama game that we'll remember forever. Solo spin-moves are fun, but as Jim says, they're only real when shared.

Connor and I were tailgating with our family before the Rams' opener in 2015. Everyone else had tickets. We did not.

"Wanna spin?" Connor asked.

"Not particularly."

"Do you wanna buy tickets?"

"I'm not paying a single cent to that slimeball." The team's owner was plotting to relocate the Rams to Los Angeles.[49]

I would love to say that more than four of my spin-moves came with a similar social agenda, if you can call it that. I would love to call myself the "Robin Hood of Sports." Team owners are greedy businessmen, commissioners are their well-compensated scapegoats, and leagues take advantage of the earnest passion of millions of fans and are tearing down the stadiums and traditions we love in the pursuit of a few more dollars.

I spin-moved Nebraska and twice at kansas because I didn't want to contribute to their schools, even though

---

49 For this game, we could've bought tickets for less than my $50 threshold, but we couldn't bring ourselves to contribute to the owner's relocation fund.

I understood: Teams and universities are all part of the same cartel. Mizzou might be Coke, kansas might be Pepsi, and it's fun to get worked up about which one is better. But their goals are the same: to convince people to drink soda.

And I spin-moved that Rams game to stick it to the owner. I'm proud to have withheld almost $9,000 from the sports industry in my spin-move career,[50] but those are the only four times I set out with that purpose.

I wanted to see a game in Buffalo one afternoon. I couldn't afford a ticket, so I hid in a garbage bin. I soon realized how much fun it was, how easy it was, and how much more I appreciated being at games after spinning. I realized that I could witness more beautiful moments — loud, passionate crowds exemplifying humanity's power when everyone's unified, pulling in the same direction — with the spin-move as my ticket.

Spin-moving became my identity; the one thing I could accomplish through sheer willpower. I thought it would make women want to talk to me. When I was depressed because it didn't, it became a sword with which I could swat away people's taunts about my being a virgin. As it turned out, those taunts were only in my head.

Maybe one out of every 10 or 15 people who've heard about the spin-move has questioned its morality. A few strangers online have called me a thief — of the experience of attending live sporting events, I suppose. But how can you steal something if no one has to relinquish it?

---

50   To estimate the get-in prices of the games I spin-moved, I used factors I remember: how much scalpers and ticket websites were charging, how much my friends paid, and the face value of tickets.

The only "victims" are profiteering owners, leagues, and ticket scalpers.

"Put yourself in the owner's shoes. How would you feel?" I've been asked.

First of all, I would be grateful to be so rich. I would want my stadium to be as loud as possible and full of the most appreciative fans. I wouldn't add extra security, just to prevent a few people from sneaking in. I would tip my cap to those who cared enough to spin, and thank them for buying tickets to hundreds of other games, for watching hundreds more on TV, and for buying all the shirts and jerseys and bumper stickers they surely own. I would also recognize that when someone sneaks into a sold-out game[51] and pays $17 for beer and peanuts, their presence is a profit.

I remember walking into a Madrid train station once. A tall man, carrying a bag of hats and soccer jerseys he had been selling on the street, looked over his shoulder at the guard's booth, saw it was empty, and without breaking stride, stepped over the turnstile.

I thought, "Damn, that was an impressive athletic display. He probably needs those two Euros he saved. Nice work, my friend." Then I swiped my ticket.

Somehow, my Super Bowl ticket forgery didn't screw over another fan. Yes, I got lucky there, but I can honestly say I've never prevented another fan from entering the stadium. I've never tripped another fan while running.

"It's against the law" is a facile argument. We don't

51   Every game I've spin-moved — minus two Rams games during their last season in St. Louis and two other games I got into just before they ended was either announced as a sell-out or actually was sold-out.

refrain from killing people because murder is illegal.
The fact that speeding is against the law doesn't stop
folks from adhering to their own, internal sense of right
and wrong when deciding how fast to drive.

Most owners don't even own their teams' stadiums.
They've built a cottage industry out of extorting hundreds of millions of dollars from cities under the threat
of relocating their teams. Too often, city and state pol-
iticians (who deserve plenty of blame, too) give in and
make taxpayers fund the construction or renovation of
stadiums, despite the clear, empirical evidence that stadiums are bad public investments.

If taxpayers fund a stadium, isn't it closer to a public
park or library — which offer free access to anyone —
than the owner's private, gated community?

I'll tell ya what: The day every team owner whose
stadium was paid for with public funds announces, "X
percent of our stadium was paid for with tax money, so
we're giving away X percent of tickets to every game.
First come, first served at the box office" ... that'll be the
day I hang up my spinning shoes for good.

"The game isn't what's important," I told Connor
as we considered spin-moving that Rams game. "The
tailgate is. We're here on a beautiful morning with our
family, drinking beer and listening to music and eating
and laughing. Remember Atlanta?"

"Atlanta" happened two years earlier.

The Mizzou football team was one of the best in the
country while I was in grad school. My friends had moved
away, and my relationships with them were beginning to

fade. But if the Tigers could keep winning and reach the SEC Championship Game in Atlanta, all of them — Jim, Al, Aaron, and dozens of others — would have to take one more road trip.

I've been nervous during games. Too nervous. Sweating. Clenching my fists. Holding my head in my hands. I've pulled hairs out of my head. I've banged my hand so hard on seats in front of me while making noise with the Tigers on defense that my knuckles bled.

But each game that season transcended sports. The Tigers had to win. Not for the normal reasons, which, come to think of it, are hard to define. They had to win so I could see my friends. And they did.

In Atlanta, I found a parking lot a mile from the stadium. I was the first one there. I told everyone where I was, and the cars started rolling in. Jim's Wagon, carrying Drew and Ben and Cody. Al's car. Aaron's truck. Connor's carload of friends from Missouri. Eric and Mike and Jeremy and Steve and Bruce. They all showed up, and with each arrival, everyone got a big hug from everyone else. We hadn't been together like that since we left college.

Those four hours, with burgers on the grill and beer sitting out because the weather was chilly enough to keep it cold, my car idling so we could play classic rock, were better than any game I've attended. Of all the memories I've made as a sports fan, all the ups and downs and heartbreaks and tears and hugs — that tailgate, all of us excited for the game but even more excited to be together — is the one I wouldn't trade for anything.

Connor nodded. "You have a point, Trev. But hey —
we're here anyway. Let's at least check it out."

I knew that tactic well. We knew that stadium well,
too: nothing behind the ticket takers except wide staircases that led to the nosebleeds.

Connor took the right side of the entrance, wiggled
through a turnstile, out of the ticket taker's grasp, and
ran up the stairs. I went to the far-left side of the entrance
and slipped through a small gap between a turnstile and
a metal barricade. We met in Section 430. "We're in,"
we said at the same time, and shook hands like old pros.
We exchanged a look and a smile that I'll never forget.

My and Connor's formative years coincided with the
Rams' years of historic ineptitude, from 2005-2015. Our
fandom was kept aflame by an image. Even with the
team miles out of the playoffs and the Dome half-empty,
that place could get really goddamn loud.

All we wanted was one home playoff game. One
chance to hear what a domed stadium, with its endless
metal railings shooting echoes in every direction, full of
frustrated, tortured football fans, might sound like in the
moments before kickoff.

We never got that chance.

The owner held the team hostage, and when he didn't
get enough ransom, he took the team we had poured our
hearts and souls into. He took my family's tailgates: our
most consistent, fun, and meaningful gatherings. The
strongest connection Mom and her two brothers had to
their father, who loved football more than anything, and
who died when he was far too young.

Fuck the owners. I regret nothing.

CHAPTER 67

I had one last look when I was in college.

I sat in the upper deck of Mizzou Arena, watching my friends graduate with big smiles on their faces. Then Michelle was announced, and I thought about the fake Super Bowl ticket in a shoebox at the back of my closet.

I wrote her a message, read it over once, and sent it.

"When I heard your name, it reminded me that I had a couple things I wanted to say … We had that one date, and although we missed the bus (and I missed my chance to be the guy with the belle of the ball on his arm), it was the best party I never went to."

I figured she was leaving town for good the next day and I would never see her again. At least I told her how I felt.

"Trevor. That's the sweetest thing anyone has ever said to me," she wrote back.

"Well, it came from the heart."

Two days later, on a beautiful Monday afternoon,

I walked around the parking garage that I usually cut through, so I could soak in an extra minute of sun. And there she was, walking right toward me.

"What, did you end up flunking or something?" I joked.

"I'm staying here this summer! I've got a job and all."

Running into her had been so sudden that I didn't have time to think and screw it up.

"We should catch up sometime … got any dinner plans tonight?" I blurted.

"Um, actually I don't."

Over burgers and beers, she mentioned, oh so casually, that she was single. We parted with a friendly hug. I walked away, unsure of whether it had been a "date." In my four-beer buzz, I turned around and swung for the fences.

"Michelle, one more thing." I approached her.

"I've always wanted to do this," I said in little more than a whisper. I kissed her. Reluctant at first, she almost imperceptibly giggled, then kissed me back.

I backpedaled and threw my arms up, exaggerating a shrug. "Just so I can say I did."

She laughed. Not a cut-the-tension laugh, but a genuine, bellyful laugh.

I turned away, and, hoping she was still watching, skipped — even danced — knowing neither where I was going nor why, only that I was on top of the world, and that my heart and my head were exploding with nerves and energy and adrenaline as sweet as any spin-move ever was.

"You never cease to surprise me," she texted.

"I fly by the seat of my pants," I responded, which was usually, but not always, false.

The next night, she came over to watch a movie and we made out during most of it. *It only takes one*, I thought. One fulfilling relationship to put to rest all the pain and the curses and the demons and the failures.

My spin-move stories have one of those tidy, full-circle endings we all crave, but you've come to the wrong place if you want a Hollywood, protagonist-gets-the-girl ending.

The next time we met, I joined Michelle and her dog for a walk in the park — a casual date seemed like a great idea. She was dropping me off at home, and the dog was sitting on my lap in the passenger seat, licking my face.

I sat there, ready to open the door and get out, trying to find the right comic wordplay about how I already got plenty of doggie kisses, so I didn't feel the need to go in for one with Michelle.

I cringe when I remember what I said. It was something like, "I want to kiss you, but I don't know if you'd be opposed, since Roxie was licking my face."

"You took a weird way to get to that," she said with a cut-the-tension laugh.

"Well, I didn't want you to think I have bad breath."

I leaned in, we pecked, and I think, right then and there, like when the crowd is going nuts late in a close game and the visiting team knocks down a 3, the air was sucked out of the building.

The next time I texted her, she said she wasn't feeling well.

"If you think some ice cream might help you feel better, let me know and I'll bring some over!"

No reply, and that was the end of the story.

I was upset, sure that my ice cream offer was too much, too soon. Too boyfriend-y after just two dates. Too intense.

But in my stronger moments, I realize: I *danced* home after that spontaneous, wing-and-a-prayer kiss.

The first sports cliché I remember hearing from Dad is, "It's not whether you win or lose, but how you play the game." I wish he had been around to remind me before I gave up on love and tried to turn myself into a machine.

I haven't watched one minute of an NFL game since January 12, 2016 — the day NFL owners voted to move the Rams to Los Angeles. I was too disgusted and too devastated to remain a fan. No Cardinals playoff loss, no Gonzaga Tournament loss, none of the creatively painful ways Mizzou has invented to lose has ever hurt worse than leaving the game entirely.

It's not whether you win or lose, but how — and *that* — you play the game. That you try. That you go all-in. And that you find meaning in it.

I didn't dance home after that kiss because it won her heart or swept her off her feet. I danced home, feeling like I would live forever, strumming the air guitar along with the music in my headphones, people looking at me like I was crazy — which I am and always will be — because I played the game. Because I played it my way. Because I played well.

A few months later, my friend Dean begged me, for my own good, to download a dating app. He sat with me for an hour, helping me choose profile pictures and describe myself. "Let's see here," I said. "Neurotic. Selfish. Sports-obsessed. I'm a real catch, eh?"

But I was already speeding down my path of giving up on the game. Those apps, and my instinct to start conversations and ask for phone numbers on trains, at bookstores, and in coffee shops remained unused for another two years or so.

There was no light-bulb moment when I decided to start trying again. Real life doesn't work that way. It was the compounding effect of night after night, lying on my bed after busy days, feeling healthy, fulfilled, and engaged with the world, listening to a great record in the dark, and wishing I could share that moment with someone.

I think I have a better outlook now.

It should've been common sense, but I got it eventually, with some help from hockey analytics. There's too much luck involved in the game to guarantee a win — no matter how much I want it. I'm not entitled to anything. I can only tilt the odds in my favor by taking more shots.

I still want to feel the warmth of a pretty woman's lips on a snowy day. I want her to nestle under my arm on a sunny day in the park after a picnic. I want her to swing her legs over my lap as we snuggle under a blanket while watching a movie in a dark apartment. I want to hold hands tenderly while we make love.

But my identity and self-esteem no longer depend on it. My dad didn't unravel because he lacked the love of a woman. That was one factor, but he was unstable all along.

I'll let the game come to me; one magical season really can make all the pain of the past worth it. If it happens, great. If not, well, sometimes you win, sometimes you lose, and sometimes it rains.

A relationship isn't necessary to complete the narrative of my life's movie; that movie is a mere figment of my imagination. I no longer need to be the guy who has it all. Baseball fans grew to hate the Cardinals because they won all the time. Nobody likes the guy who has it all.

At my 25th birthday dinner, Pop was reminiscing about Dad. "It was those teenage years. Something just … went wrong. He started taking everything so seriously. He started letting his emotions get the best of him. But somehow," he said to my mom's mom, "Bryan got himself together enough to go up to your daughter and introduce himself … and now we have these guys." He gestured to me and Connor as his eyes filled with tears.

For a while, Dad was loved by and in love with an amazing woman, who became an amazing mother to their children. He had a job he was good at and hobbies that fulfilled him. For a while, he was happy, healthy, and productive.

Can I become *that version* of him?

Here's a start: I take complete responsibility for every single one of my actions and thoughts. And I wouldn't change a thing. Not a comma in a text message, not Venice or its aftermath, not my failed spin at La Bombonera. I wouldn't have a story to tell if I hadn't made so many mistakes.

I no longer believe in the Hollywood version of love. I've got myself pretty well convinced that the institution of marriage, the nuclear family, and the glorification of home ownership are forms of societally encouraged domestication. I've had sexual opportunities, but I still worry they'll be hollow without a real commitment. I've liked a few women enough to pursue a long-term relationship, but one smoked too much; one drank too much; one is married. And I've seen relationships turn too many friends into less adventurous and less interesting shells of their former selves to get involved in anything that doesn't feel right.

Maybe I'm rationalizing. My expectations and standards are probably still too high. Maybe I haven't grown up since I was a freshman in college. But if surrendering the ability to drop everything and hit the road — if sacrificing the freedom to be whoever, whatever, wherever I want — is "growing up," then I want no part of it.

So maybe the better question is: Can I deal with the ups and downs of the real world for longer — much longer — than Dad did? Can I keep enduring rejection and frustration and use the pain to make me stronger? Can I show up to a movie theater, realize there's gum on the floor or the armrest is broken, and just … let it be?

There's no opponent to outhustle. The bounces and calls won't always go my way.

There are no tickets for sale.

But I'll come up with something.

CHAPTER 68

As I write these words, the last true spin-move took place in October of 2016.

I drove to the Chicago suburbs to see a friend on the day the Cubs had a chance to win the Pennant.

If they won, World Series Games 3, 4, and 5 — but neither Game 6 nor 7 — would be played in Chicago. The odds were therefore against them winning it all at home. I wanted to see a celebration at Wrigley. And, as Dad said, we tend to celebrate a win that keeps the season going more than a win that ends it.

My friend, Kevin, invited me to lunch with his grandparents: passionate Cubs fans their entire lives.

"We hear you're some sort of trickster," his grandfather said.

"Yeah, sneaking into games is one of my hobbies."

His grandma laughed. "Well, we wish you the best of luck."

"Thank you, I'll need it. How do you two feel about this game tonight?"

I remembered a story Dad loved to tell. When he was a teenager, he and his dad were eating dinner on a summer evening on which the Cardinals weren't playing. "Man, nights without ballgames feel ... empty," Pop said.

Once upon a time, Pop listened to every Cardinals game on the radio. He had Blues season tickets. He had been a diehard, like me, Dad, and Connor. But the ups and downs — the heart-pounding, nail-biting stress of sports fandom — became too much for him.

"I *hate* overtime," Pop said once, after a Blues playoff game. "Feels like I'm gonna have a heart attack. I just want them to get it over with so I can turn off the TV."

He settled into a routine of novels and classical music, light workouts, card games, and arguments about minutiae with friends at the local health club. Every morning, he spreads butter on a toasted slice of French baguette, covers it with blackberry preserves, and reads the sports section. A mellow life, lived on an even keel.

In Chicago, Kevin's grandfather said, "Oh," with a sigh, then looked to the ceiling for a second, before looking back at me. "We sure want the Cubs to win."

Maybe his wrinkles had blunted the expression in his face. I couldn't tell if he was understating his feelings. Maybe what he meant to say was, "I want them to win

with every fiber of my being. I'm 86 goddamn years old
and my nerves might kill me tonight."

Or, maybe age had tempered his nerves. Maybe
sports didn't mean to him what they once did. Maybe he
had grown calmer as he grew older and realized there
are more important things in life than baseball.

I wish Dad could have lived long enough to become
his dad, but do I want the same even keel for myself? If
I live as long as Pop, I might not have a choice; Father
Time is throwing a perfect game. For now, though, while
my heart can handle them, give me the ups and downs.
Nothing means anything if your heart's not on the line.

I asked my buddy's grandparents, "Do you have any
particularly strong memories, anything that stands out,
after all these years?"

"I could never forget Bill Nicholson. They called him
Swish. No one ever looked so good striking out," Kevin's
grandma said. Her husband smiled and agreed.

They remembered not the pain of any loss, nor the joy
of any win, but a tiny detail of the journey. An inside joke.

When we finished our sandwiches, I drove toward
Wrigley Field, the old ballpark with the cramped concourses and troughs in the bathrooms — the way it's
supposed to be. The house of horrors. The shrine to
lovable loserdom.

The Red Sox and White Sox broke their droughts on
the road. No drought in the NBA or NHL has ever come
close. Super Bowls, Final Fours, and College Football
National Championship Games are at neutral sites.

Wrigley was about to host the most emotional crowd
and the greatest moment in North American sports

history: the moment that would put to rest 71 years without a Pennant.

I took my lap around the outside. There were no turnstiles at the entrances, but they were so crowded, I couldn't get a clean view of the ticket takers — or whatever was behind them.

Jim, who's from Chicago, met me at the Harry Caray statue.

"I sure needed to see a friendly face," I said.

"What's wrong? You're never uptight in these situations."

"I'm not sure about this one. Lots of uncertainty."

"Let's have a look. I have some ideas."

We walked around the ballpark again, the two of us scheming like the old days. First pitch was in 40 minutes.

"I would do the right-field entrance." Jim pointed at it. "More options. You can run straight and hide in the bleachers, or you can go left or right."

"Yeah, but I can't actually see what's behind the ticket takers. Over by the first-base entrance, at least I can kinda see. At least I can go up there with a plan."

On the right side of that entrance was a staircase leading to the upper deck.

Jim knew what I needed to hear, and almost nothing is more valuable than a friend who knows you that well.

"Then trust your instincts. This is your thing. Maybe the one thing you were put on this earth to do. The one thing where you can legitimately say you're the best in the world."

I wasn't thinking about that. I just wanted to bring the spin-move full circle. We walked back toward the first-base entrance — Gate D at Wrigley Field — where it all began, 11 years and a lifetime earlier, when a father and his sons just wanted to see a ballgame on a rainy weekend afternoon.

I hopped a couple of times, stretched my legs, clapped my hands, and glared at Jim with my game face, like a tennis player looking at his coach in the stands. "It's time," I said. "You sure you don't wanna come?"

"Nah, I'm just here for moral support. I wanna watch you spin, and then I'm heading to the bar. If we lose tonight, I'll do Game 7 with you." We hugged.

I put my wallet and phone in the plastic box and walked through the metal detector on the left side of Gate D. The ticket takers stood in a line that spanned the whole gate.

Stadium security guards in green jackets lurked behind the ticket takers on the left side. However, behind the ticket takers to the *right*, there was nothing except that concrete staircase.

Each ticket in my collection of stubs tells its own story; I didn't want to use one of those as my decoy. So I'd Googled "PDF baseball ticket" and printed a paper copy from a Toronto Blue Jays game two years earlier. I folded it so that only the barcode was showing. I handed it to the ticket taker directly in front of the staircase. She took it in her hand.

She was almost shoulder-to-shoulder with the ticket taker next to her. Had I run, I would've run her over, so I turned sideways to make myself as thin as possible and shuffled past.

"Whoa, sir!" she said as I went, and I felt a pair of

hands on my jacket. I kept moving and got away. I danced around a fan at the foot of the stairs, then took three steps at a time. I turned the corner and went up another flight. Then another. Then another, with confused fans watching me, wondering why the hell I was running.

At the top, I cut left behind the lower-level seats. I took the ramps to the upper deck, took off my jacket, and texted Jim: "I'm in."

"Tried to set up my phone to get a video. When I looked up, you were gone."

The building shook with every run the Cubs scored. They led 5-0 late in the game. It was going to happen. Every out was its own miniature celebration. The ovation for Kyle Hendricks, who twirled a two-hitter over 7 and 1/3 innings, was the loudest cheer of all.

This was not my party. As self-righteous, bandwagony, and hateable as the Cardinals and their fanbase have become, they are my grandpa's team, my dad's team, my uncles' team, my mom's, my grandma's. They are my brother's team, and damnit, they're my team, too, and in 50 years, when Connor and I are old men, we'll sit in the upper deck and talk about how Dad wanted us to love each other, and how he gave us this thing to bond over called sports. Then we'll talk about John Mabry, Steve Kline, and Kent Bottenfield — the Bill Nicholsons of our childhood. And we'll laugh.

I stood still and silent when the Cubs turned a double play to end it. I watched the mass of blue in the stands jump as one, before losing the rhythm and becoming chaos — thousands of waves crashing into each other, celebrating. Going nuts.

"Go Cubs Go" blared from the speakers, but I was listening to "A Dying Cub Fan's Last Request" in my mind. With tears in my eyes, I watched the iconic 'W' flag rise, as it does after every Cubs win at Wrigley Field. The Cubs were not my team, but the Lovable Loser was my story.

And sports fandom is my identity. It has been the source of more misery and frustration than I can remember, but it has also brought me to London and San Francisco and Spokane; to friends' houses, to my feet in excitement, to my knees in disbelief, and into my brother's arms, both in elation and in pain. It brought me Albert's homer in '05, the Zags' blown lead in '06, and everything in between. The whole emotional spectrum. Isn't that the point?

Sports fandom had led me there, to witness that singular moment in history. It had proven that the longer you wait for something, and the more pain it causes, and the more desperately you want it, the better it feels when it happens. And that, therefore, I'm not crazy for loving to lose.

The desire for that moment had united millions of people and inspired thousands of dreams — kids in the backyard pretending to be at-bat in the bottom of the ninth with the Cubs one swing away from winning the Pennant.

But then it actually happened. I closed my eyes and tried to burn the image of euphoria into my brain, so I could replay it anywhere, anytime. So it would last forever.

329

When I left the stadium, I saw individual people, packed against each other with no room to move, shuffling along quietly. I saw their eyes. They were dry. I saw their faces. They were blank. They had already moved on to the next thing — to the next series, to the next bill they had to pay, to the fact that the streets were mobbed, and they had nowhere to pee.

The desire, the struggle, the pursuit, and the anticipation of winning the Pennant lasted 71 years. The joy — the true, all-in joy of winning — lasted half an hour.

Two weeks later, the Cubs won the World Series in Cleveland as I watched from my couch, with peanut shells and empty beer bottles on the floor around me. Two days after that, I watched coverage of the parade in Chicago. It showed people jumping on each other's backs and clambering to get in front of the cameras, trying to recreate a moment that had passed.

I tried to transport myself back to the moment I saw the Cubs win the Pennant. I had it for a second, but the edges began to fade, it became blurry, and then, like sand slipping through cupped hands, it trickled away.

In its place appeared an old ballpark, half-empty, an hour before the game, on a rainy weekend afternoon. The Friendly Confines, after sneaking in with my dad and brother.

Wrigley Field, when I saw it for the first time.

EXTRA INNINGS

If you leave an honest review of *Ticketless* on Amazon, email me at trevor@ticketless.pub with the subject "FRIEND" so I can send you exclusive bonus content — summaries and highlights of the games I spin-moved (in the style of the four I've included here); eight spin-move stories that aren't in the book; dozens more photos of security setups; research into the colorful history of sports gatecrashing; and my thoughts on its murky future.

And if you've ever snuck into a sporting event (or anywhere else interesting), please reach out to me. With your permission, I'd love to feature the best stories in future writings.

1. AUGUST 13, 2005: CARDINALS 5, CUBS 2.

WRIGLEY FIELD, CHICAGO, IL

Get-in Price: Approximately $100. Scalpers were offering tickets for $150, but Dad was a good negotiator.

The start of this game was rain-delayed by two hours and 42 minutes. That was fine with us; we had more time to take in Wrigley Field.

Albert hit his 33rd home run of the season into the basket in right field, and the ball stayed there the rest of the game. Chris Carpenter tossed a complete game, striking out eight. The Cards went to 74-43 and increased their lead in the division to 10.5 games.

Dad was ... Dad. When we got to the bleachers in the seventh inning, we sat behind a guy in a Cubs hat with the tag still on, which I guess was some kind of fashion statement at the time. Dad didn't get it, and that tag just ... kept ... bothering him. When he mentioned it to a fellow Cardinals fan sitting next to us, he offered Dad $10 to yank the tag off.

Dad took the money, pulled the tag off, then shrugged, apologized, and gave $5 to the guy with the hat. "Here, you can buy a new one," Dad said. "I just couldn't stand that thing flopping around."

I had never caught a foul ball or a home run (and still haven't — I shit you not, I currently despise my foul ball virginity almost as much as I used to despise my actual virginity). After the game, I made Dad angry when I wandered off to retrieve Albert's homer from the basket without telling him where I was going. The ball was gone by the time I got there.

11. OCTOBER 28, 2011: CARDINALS 6, RANGERS 2.

BUSCH STADIUM, ST. LOUIS, MO

Get-in Price: I remember St. Louis police cracking down on scalping (which is technically illegal) before Game 7. Apparently, there were reports of folks selling paperclips for $500, then "giving away" a ticket to the game to avoid legal consequences.

Game 6 is the one everybody remembers; it's gone down as one of the greatest games of all time. The truth is, it was a poorly pitched, sloppy, error-filled game — until the bottom of the ninth inning. With the Cardinals trailing the series 3-2, two outs, down to their last strike, St. Louis-born-and-raised David Freese (who had dropped two pop-ups) hit a game-tying triple.

Again down to their last strike in the 10th, Lance Berkman tied it with a single. Freese won it in the 11th with a solo homer.

I considered spinning Game 6. Deciding against it still haunts me. I had a test early the next day, but the real reason I didn't go is that if the Cardinals lost, I wouldn't have wanted to see the Rangers celebrate on our field. If the Cards won, I would spin Game 7, which I figured would be more dramatic anyway. Little did I know I'd miss three of the greatest moments in baseball history.

As the professor was handing out the test packets the morning after Game 6, I raised my hand. "Professor, probably half the class is from the St. Louis area, and the Cardinals played a pretty important game last night ... I don't see how any of us could really have studied effectively. What do you think about postponing the test until Monday?"

He looked away and responded, "Does anyone *else* have a question?" Another student raised his hand. "Well, this is probably a dumb question but … " the professor cut him off. "There's no such thing as a dumb question — except the one about postponing a test for baseball."

At the end of the semester, my grade dangling between B and B+, I emailed the professor:

"I truly believe that my grade on Test 2 was significantly worse than it would've been had it been taken at any time other than 9:00 a.m. the day after the greatest baseball game of all time was played. I was half-joking in class when I asked you to push the test back, because I knew the logistics of it would be hard to manage, but nonetheless, my nerves were frayed after that game, and even though I had studied beforehand, almost everything I had studied went right out the window with all the drama of that Game 6. And after the game, I certainly wasn't in any position to continue studying."

Unbeknownst to me, I had my B+; the professor had announced on the class website that he would curve the final exam. He responded to my email, "Trevor, read the announcement I posted. I think you will find it enlightening. Then ponder the following quote: 'It is better to remain silent and be thought a fool than to open one's mouth and remove all doubt.' Best wishes for the holidays."

I thought about it for a while, then responded, "Professor, my deepest, most sincere apologies for not noticing your announcement. A quote for you to ponder: 'If you can't say anything nice, don't say anything at all.' Merry Christmas and Happy Hanukkah."

Anyway, at Game 7, Connor and I watched from a standing-room-only area along the first-base line. The Rangers scored two in the top of the first, but Freese hit a two-run double in the bottom half to tie it. Chris Carpenter settled in, Arthur Rhodes and Octavio Dotel were solid in relief, and the Cardinals scratched across runs in the third, fifth, and seventh to win their 11th World Series.

The Blues lost 3-1 in Calgary.

28. DECEMBER 17, 2015: RAMS 31, BUCCANEERS 23.

EDWARD JONES DOME, ST. LOUIS, MO

NOT INCLUDED IN THE NARRATIVE OF TICKETLESS

Get-in Price: No joke, we might've been able to get tickets for $5 apiece.

The Rams were 5-8 heading into this, their final home game of the season. Connor and I attended the Blues-Predators game (with tickets) that same Thursday night. Knowing there was a good chance it would be the last-ever Rams game in St. Louis, we drove to the Dome after the hockey game to catch the fourth quarter.

As we jogged toward the stadium, we asked fans walking the other way if we could have their ticket stubs. Eventually, we got two. We didn't need them. We walked into the stadium's veranda and saw that the turnstiles had been dragged to the side. The few security guards and ushers who were in the area seemed singularly focused on making sure no one left the building with beer still in their cups (which would be a liability for the team).

We put our heads down and walked in. Someone probably saw us — and didn't care. We met up with our family in a half-empty Section 406, where we'd spent so many Sunday afternoons.

I remember being angry at the people who just stood up and left as the clock wound down. This was potentially the Rams' last game in St. Louis! On that night, the game was not the main event. The *atmosphere* was: the looks on people's faces; the anger and the passion in their voices; the moment of confused melancholy when the clock hit 0:00.

Some fans did stay after the final whistle and made their way down to the lower level, near the NFL Network's post-game set. The heroes of the Rams' glory days, Marshall Faulk and Kurt Warner, were part of the crew, and it felt like we fans were begging them to do something, anything in their power, to help us. "Keep the Rams!" was the chant.

We briefly drowned out the TV crew when the chant became, "Kroenke sucks! Kroenke sucks!" — which remains a St. Louis staple, especially when the Blues host the Kroenke-owned Colorado Avalanche.

I wrote in my journal, "Connor and I took one last look around, just in case it was the last time. I wasn't 'sad,' just stunned momentarily. I guess that would be the best way to describe it. So many Sundays spent there, lots of great family moments, lots of laughs … just not very good football. And that's ok. I just wanted to hear the Dome at full capacity one time. But the best things never happen … or they tease you for a long fucking time until they do."

29. OCTOBER 22, 2016: CUBS 5, DODGERS 0.

WRIGLEY FIELD, CHICAGO, IL

Get-in Price: My friend Eric paid $330 to sit in the bleachers for Game 2 of this series. For the Pennant clincher, I'd be surprised if anyone could've paid less than $700 on the secondary market.

Clayton Kershaw, a surefire, future hall-of-famer, was on the bump with the Dodgers facing elimination. The Cubs jumped all over him in the bottom of the first. Dexter Fowler doubled. Kris Bryant singled to drive him in. The Dodgers' Andrew Toles dropped a fly ball in left field, and Ben Zobrist hit a sac-fly for a 2-0 lead after one. The Cubs added three more runs against Kershaw, and Kyle Hendricks was dynamite in 7 and 1/3 innings for the North Siders.

The ushers at Wrigley are notoriously strict, so I knew not to get on their bad side by standing in the aisles. During the first inning, I asked some guys who were standing in front of their seats in the last row of the upper deck, "Hey, mind if I squeeze in?" They said no.

I stayed on the move for the rest of the game, watching from a few different obstructed-view, standing-room areas until the ninth inning, when the ushers gave up. I found a nice spot in an upper-level walkway behind home plate.

The roar after each Cubs run shook Wrigley Field. The ovation for Hendricks, as he walked off the mound, was even louder. When the Cubs turned the double play — Russell to Baez to Rizzo — that won their first Pennant in 71 years, I was watching the crowd. That moment was beautiful, but fleeting. It was beautiful *because* it was fleeting.

THE ORIGINAL SPIN-MOVE: CARDINALS AT CUBS

In 2005, the Cubs were building the patio you see on the left. As I remember it, the ramp between the "Bag Inspection" gate and that patio was our route into the ballpark.

THE GARBAGE BIN IN BUFFALO:
FLORIDA ST. VS. GONZAGA

We pulled back the curtain on the left...

saw this garbage bin ...

then looked inside.

PAY HEED, ALL WHO ENTER: MISSOURI AT KANSAS

The kU interns in charge of handing out media credentials were
seated at a table along the wall.

The concourse beyond that table. I walked past the interns, veered
right, and just kept going.

WORLD SERIES GAME 2: RANGERS AT CARDINALS

I ran past an usher in the far-left aisle of this entrance. As the sign
says, it's a re-entry gate — primarily for smokers.

**WORLD SERIES GAME 7 AND NLCS GAME 5:
RANGERS AND GIANTS AT CARDINALS**

Connor and I, then Patrick and I the following year, waited with
our backs to the glass, the doors on our left. Both times, luckily,
it was the far door that opened. If the near door had opened, it
would've smushed us.

We ran up these stairs, which led to the upper deck.

BUSTED: SABRES AT BLUES

The exit-only doors, which Bruce opened for me, and the stairs we
would have sprinted up ... had we not been caught.

No handles on the outside of those doors, obviously.

PAY HEED, ALL WHO ENTER, PT. 2:
MISSOURI AT KANSAS

The bridge that connected the parking garage to the Allen Fieldhouse
entrances we spin-moved.

The view from the parking garage of the upper-level entrance. I got a walking start toward the ticket taker who stood toward the left as I approached. The doors were propped open, and the ticket taker was in front of them — standing on the bridge, not in the arena — which gave me more room to run past.

The concourse beyond those doors.

LIFE IS LIKE A BOX OF CHOCOLATES:
FLUMINENSE AT BOCA JUNIORS

From right to left as you look at this picture, you can see the media
entrance, which would have been a treacherous spin; Gate 9, Gate 8,
Gate 7, and, around the corner, Gate 6.

Credit: Google Earth

This photo shows, from left to right, Gates 7, 8, 9, and the media entrance. Metal barriers extended about 20 feet outward from the pillars that separate the gates from each other. After the first-layer policeman had ripped up my fake ticket at Gate 9, and because Gate 6 (not pictured) looked like the security hub, while Gate 8 was sandwiched by the other two, Gate 7 became my only option. The row of turnstiles was situated on that first step, and I was able to walk up to the stadium's wall, parallel with the turnstiles. There was a small gap between the turnstile nearest me and that pillar. I damn near pulled it off.

Credit: Google Earth

SLEEPLESS IN SEATTLE: SAINTS AT SEAHAWKS

If you look to the left, you can see a closed gate. Before the game, it was open and lined with turnstiles, ticket takers, security guards, and cops. But the doors on the right took me behind those layers of security.

MASTER(S)PIECE: AUGUSTA NATIONAL GOLF CLUB

Gate 6A. Security guards stood behind the rectangular podiums, ostensibly verifying that each patron had a badge. The sign attached to the pole says, "Please Have Badge In Hand."

In the foreground, the counter behind which the ticket taker sat. In the background, the side-by-side metal detectors that were the second layer of security.

THE HOLY FLANNEL: BRUINS AT CANADIENS

Look behind the man wearing a hat and Canadiens jersey on the left
of this photo. The man near the doors with his head down, facing
away from us, is the ticket taker I ran past — twice. The first time,
I realized almost too late that I shouldn't keep moving; the crowd
in front of me was too dense. To my right was that pillar (adorned
with advertisements) you see in the middle of the photo. To my left
were more ticket takers and security guards. So I turned around and
slipped between the ticket taker and the pillar.

THE TUNNEL BENEATH TOBACCO ROAD:
NORTH CAROLINA AT DUKE

The "secret" tunnel that led from the auxiliary gym into Cameron
Indoor Stadium.

At the end of that tunnel were two staircases: a concrete one, then a carpeted one.

The view from the top of that second staircase. The doors straight ahead took me to ...

... the courtside bleachers at Cameron Indoor.

THE FINAL OPENING DAY: SEAHAWKS AT RAMS

This is a screenshot of a poorly executed video I took of my spin-move at the Rams' final Opening Day in St. Louis. I slipped between the turnstile and the metal fence to the left. Then I ran around the fence and up the stairs, which are to the left of what this photo shows.

71 YEARS IN THE MAKING: DODGERS AT CUBS

I got past the ticket takers who were lined up along Gate D and ran up the stairs. I wanted to spin Gate D in 2016 because I had spun it with my dad and brother in 2005. And after a lap around Wrigley, it became clear: Gate D was also, by far, my best bet.

THE SPIN-MOVE CODE

I haven't followed them strictly, but here are the ground rules I laid out to keep the spin-move special.

- If I already have a ticket to a game, I can't sell it, in order to spin — no matter how much it could fetch from a scalper, and no matter how lax the security setup. Spin-moving is not about profit; it's about the thrill. It's about the bond — the memory — it creates among friends. It's about making the game mean more.
- However, if I know someone who would appreciate being at the game, but can't afford a ticket, I would feel good about giving mine away and then spinning.
- I reserve spinning for unique games. If I can buy a ticket for $50 or less, the game doesn't warrant a spin. If I can't say about a game, "That crowd is gonna be absolutely bonkers," it's not worth it.

- But when the Rams' owner was threatening to relocate the team, I spin-moved two games that didn't meet those criteria — as a middle finger to him.
- The only "victims" of the spin-move should be the league and the team owner — never another fan.
- Some games, like the first time I got to attend a Gonzaga home game, are too special to spin. If one of my teams were on the verge of winning its first championship of my lifetime, that game would be ineligible. There is no way in hell I'll be sitting in a holding cell — on the off chance I got caught — if the Blues ever skate around the ice with the Stanley Cup.

ACKNOWLEDGEMENTS

Ticketless would not have been possible without my book coach, editor, marketer, and friend, Matt Rudnitsky. Somehow, he never grew tired of telling me to *dig deeper*. If you have a great idea for a book, I hope you'll reach out to him through his company, Platypus Publishing: info@plat.pub or visit www.plat.pub for more details.

My test readers had a difficult task: I told them I needed brutal honesty. They gave it. Tony, Jackie, Catie, Adam, Silvy, Susie, Jordan, Cooper, Hildy, Andrew, John — thank you.

Jim and Dean, you guys are the best. I can only hope you'll be this supportive of my next book.

Made in the USA
Columbia, SC
15 August 2020

16481707R00219